DOWSING
for BEGINNERS

ABOUT THE AUTHOR

Richard Webster was born in New Zealand in 1946, where he still resides, though he travels widely every year lecturing and conducting workshops on psychic subjects around the world. He has written many books, mainly on psychic subjects, and also writes monthly magazine columns.

Richard is married with three children. His family is very supportive of Richard's occupation, but his oldest son, after watching his father's career, has decided to become an accountant.

DOWSING
for BEGINNERS

How to find Water,
Wealth, and Lost Objects

Richard Webster

Llewellyn Publications
Woodbury, Minnesota

FIRST EDITION
Tenth Printing, 2010

Cover design: Adrienne Zimiga
Cover images: © John Glover/Alamy
Book design, layout, and editing: Laura Gudbaur
Interior illustrations: Carla Shale
Photos: Richard Webster and Jeff Martin

Library of Congress Cataloging-in-Publication Data
Webster, Richard, 1946—
    Dowsing for beginners: The art of discovering: Water, Treasure, Gold, Oil, Artifacts / by Richard Webster.
        p. cm. --
    Includes bibliographical references and index.
    ISBN 13: 978-1-56718-802-8
    ISBN 10: 1-56718-802-8 (pbk.)
    1. Dowsing I. Title. II Series.
BF1628.W394 1996   95-49696
133.3'23--dc20   CIP

Llewellyn Publications
A division of Llewellyn Worldwide, Ltd.
2143 Wooddale Drive, Dept. 978-1-56718-802-8
Woodbury, Minnesota, 55125-2989
www.llewellyn.com
Llewellyn is a registered trademark of Llewellyn Worldwide, Ltd.
Printed in the United States of America

OTHER BOOKS BY RICHARD WEBSTER

101 Feng Shui Tips for Your Home
Astral Travel for Beginners
Aura Reading for Beginners
Candle Magic for Beginners
Color Magic for Beginners
Creative Visualization for Beginners
The Encyclopedia of Angels
The Encyclopedia of Superstitions
Feng Shui for Apartment Living
Feng Shui for Beginners
Feng Shui for Success & Happiness
Feng Shui for Your Apartment
Feng Shui in the Garden
Flower and Tree Magic
Gabriel
How to Write for the New Age Market
Is Your Pet Psychic?
Magical Symbols of Love & Romance
Michael
Miracles
Palm Reading for Beginners
Pendulum Magic for Beginners
Practical Guide to Past-Life Memories
Prayer for Beginners
Praying with Angels
Psychic Protection for Beginners
Raphael
Soul Mates
Spirit Guides & Angel Guardians
Success Secrets
Uriel
Write Your Own Magic
You Can Read Palms

DEDICATION

For my fellow members of the New Zealand Society of Dowsing and Radionics (Inc.)

ACKNOWLEDGEMENTS

I am grateful to many people who have helped me over the years with my interest in dowsing. In particular I'd like to thank Jack Camp, Brian and Jan Flora, Albino Gola, Carl Herron, Docc and Caroline Hilford, Walter Lemm, Jim and Melania Magus, Jeff Martin and Ron Martin.

Contents

# Introduction

One of the fascinating things about dowsing is that virtually everyone can do it, provided they are prepared to suspend disbelief.

I have proven this numerous times in my own classes. Many people experience a dowsing response right away, and are enthralled with their success. Some, however, fail to get any response. I ask these people to pretend that they can dowse. To their amazement, they find that by imagining they can do it, they really can. Their expressions of surprise and disbelief are a joy to behold.

Consequently, I know that you can become a successful dowser. Naturally, it will take time and practice, but if you are prepared to keep an open mind as you work your way through this book, I am confident that you will become a very good dowser.

My introduction to dowsing came as a small boy. We were spending the summer vacation in a cottage at a small seaside village. One day during lunch, we heard a noise outside. We looked out the window and saw a man with a forked stick walking onto our property. A small crowd of people followed him. We raced outside to join the others, having no idea what the man was doing. Our next-door neighbor approached the man and asked him what he wanted.

"Water. Water," he said in a croaky voice. Our neighbor disappeared and returned moments later with a glass of water.

This broke the spell. The man suddenly realized the attention he had created and hurriedly left. The group continued to talk about the strange man and his wooden rod. While this was going on, my father returned from a fishing trip and asked what was happening.

"He was dowsing!" my father said to everyone. He had to explain what it was and everyone drifted away, embarrassed that they had not known what the man was doing.

This man started something, though. During the next few weeks we saw many of the other holiday-makers experimenting at water-divining. My father met the man who had started it all, and we all tried divining with his makeshift rod. All four of us children found it easy to do, and, because it was so easy, we left it to the adults while we got on with our games.

It took me another fifteen years before I became interested in the pendulum and started dowsing seriously.

Dowsing can be described as divining for something that is desired. Most people consider dowsing to be a search for water, and this is how the whole field began thousands of years ago. However, you can divine for anything you want, be it oil, gold, lead, or even ancient ruins. You can find missing people or lost objects. You can determine if something is safe to eat or drink. I have seen people dangling a pendulum over fruit in the supermarket, but I feel that this is taking it a little too far! I have even met a few people who dowse for the winners of horse races.[1]

Dowsing has a very ancient history. There are pictographs in the Tassili-n-Ajjer caves in south-east Libya that show a group of people watching a diviner with a forked stick. It has been estimated that these drawings could be 8,000 years old.

In the fifth century B.C., Herodotus described how the Scythians dowsed with willow rods. There is a tradition that suggests that the Queen of Sheba included dowsers in her entourage whenever she traveled to see Solomon. Their task was to dowse for water and gold.

Divining "rods" are mentioned several times in the Old Testament. In the Book of Numbers (XX:8–11), Moses is said to have struck a rock twice with his rod, and the rock produced enough water to satisfy Moses' people and their cattle. Rods were considered acceptable in the Old Testament only if they were used for the Lord's work.[2] They can be related today to the bishop's staff and the sorcerer's magic wand.

The Catholic church disapproved of any form of divination, so for many years dowsing was considered to be the work of the devil. Martin Luther also regarded dowsing as a mortal sin, and even included it in his list of activities that broke the first commandment. This is rather strange, as Martin Luther was the son

**Figure A: Woodcut from *Cosmographia Universalis*,
by Sebastian Münster (1544)**

of a miner, and must have been well aware that dowsing rods were used constantly in mines.

In the sixteenth century, dowsing rods were regularly used in German mines. In 1546, Georgius Agricola published *De Re Metallica (On Metals)*, a book on mining, which explained in detail the necessity of the divining rod in finding and exploring mines.[3] This book was encyclopedic in scope and became the standard textbook on mining for at least a century afterwards. Its importance was such that copies were chained in churches, just like Bibles, and the priests would read from it to the illiterate miners.

Georgius Agricola was the doctor at a mining camp in northern Bohemia. He became fascinated with mining and mining lore, and his famous book recounts all he learned. There is an engraving in this book that shows two prospectors dowsing, while a third is cutting a branch from a tree to make a rod. These German dowsers later brought their skill to England to help the locals divine for tin in Devon and Cornwall. Queen Elizabeth I actively encouraged these miners to come to England to locate and exploit the country's mineral resources.

The first person to write about dowsing in English was Robert Boyle, often called the Father of Chemistry. Although he had been unsuccessful in his own attempts to dowse, he remained open-minded on the subject. In an essay published in 1661 he wrote:

> *A forked hazel twig is held by its horns, one in each hand, the holder walking with it over places where mineral lodes may be suspected, and it is said that the fork by dipping down will discover the place where the ore is to be found. Many eminent authors, amongst others our distinguished countryman Gabriel Plat, ascribe much to this detecting wand, far from credulous or ignorant, have as eye-witnesses spoken of its value. When visiting the lead-mines of Somerset-*

*shire I saw its use, and one gentleman who
employed it declared that it moved without his
will, and I saw it bend so strongly as to break in
his hand. It will only succeed in some men's
hands, and those who have seen it may much
more readily believe than those who have not.*[4]

In the late sixteenth century, a girl, Martine de
Bertereau, was born who grew up to become the first
famous dowser. She was married to a leading mining
expert, Baron de Beausoleil et d'Auffenbach. She
gained her interest in dowsing from him, and
became an expert at divining minerals as well as
water. Her discovery of the Château-Thierry mineral springs in 1629 was just one of many achieve-
ments that led her to become a mining advisor to the
French government.[5]

She was hundreds of years ahead of her time. Flu-
ent in three languages and possessing an extremely
adventurous nature and a constant wanderlust, she
must have been stimulating company. She traveled
extensively, even across the Atlantic to Bolivia, where
she examined the gold mines high up in the Andes.

Unfortunately, her interest in dowsing was con-
strued by many as being associated with witchcraft,
and she and her husband were arrested in 1627. The
baron was able to successfully defend the charges, but
their dowsing equipment, mineral samples, maps,
reports, and a large sum of money were not returned.
The couple moved to Germany. They appeared to
prosper again until 1640 when the baroness published a book called *La Restitution de Pluton*. In this
book she described her dowsing instruments. This

Figure B: 16th century German woodcut

provided her enemies with the ammunition they needed. The baron and baroness were imprisoned in different prisons, and both died there.[6]

The first English book on dowsing was *A Discovery of Subterraneall Treasure,* by Gabriel Plattes, which was published in 1639. It did not take long for the skeptics to become involved. Just seven years later Sir Thomas Browne classified dowsing as an illusion in *Pseudodoxia Epidemica.*

Despite the regular use of rods in mining, up until the end of the seventeenth century dowsers were constantly at risk of being charged with witchcraft.

Gradually, this changed, partly due to the abilities of a young French dowser named Jacques Aymar. For ten years the French press was full of stories of his amazing feats. He had already achieved a considerable local reputation with his ability at tracking down villains. However, it was not until 1692, when he was twenty-nine, that he achieved European fame. That year he successfully located one of the murderers of a wine merchant and his wife.

The murder was a particularly brutal one, and the gendarmes found no clues at all in the wine cellar where the murders took place. In desperation, the king's procurator summoned Aymar, as he was renowned for his ability at finding criminals.

Aymar used his forked stick in the cellar and told the police the exact location of the murders. Then he took to the streets, followed by a crowd of interested onlookers. Unfortunately, his path led him to one of the city gates which had been locked for the night, so the chase had to be postponed until the next day.

The following morning, Aymar and three gendarmes followed a river until they came to a small gardener's cottage. Inside was an empty wine bottle. His dowsing rod reacted strongly to it, and also to the table and three of the chairs. Aymar confidently told the gendarmes that they were after three men, and they had stopped here long enough to consume the bottle of wine. This finding was confirmed by the gardener's two small children.

Aymar and the gendarmes continued their chase. The dowsing rod took them all the way to a prison in the town of Beaucaire. Thirteen recently-arrested prisoners were lined up, and Aymar's rod reacted in front of one them, a hunchback who had been jailed just one hour earlier. Aymar told the gendarmes that this man had played a minor role in the murders.

The man denied any knowledge of the crime, but later broke down and confessed after being recognized by people on the return trip to Lyon. This man was actually a servant of the two men who had committed the murders, and had been employed to help carry the gold and silver stolen from the victims.

The procurator was pleased with Aymar's work and commissioned him to find the real villains. Accompanied by a group of archers, Aymar finished up in the port of Toulon where he was just one day too late. The two murderers had left by boat for Genoa in Italy the previous day. Aymar became a hero, but many people were concerned that dowsing could lead to grave injustices if guilt and innocence were to be determined by a rod.[7]

Several books were written arguing whether or not demons inhabited dowsing rods. Even the procurator wrote a book about Jacques Aymar's feat called *Histoire merveilleuse d'un macon qui, conduit par la baguette divinatoire, a suivi un meurtrier pendant 45 heures sur la terre et plus 30 heures sur l'eau*. For a while dowsing became a popular method of tracking down criminals, but because of natural doubts about the reliability of this method, the French courts banned it by official decree in 1701.

During the eighteenth century, dowsing quietly flourished in many countries. Colonial settlers in the United States made great use of dowsing to irrigate new areas as they expanded across the continent.[8] In 1725, *La Physique occulte ou traité de la baguette divinatoire,* by Abbé de Vallemont, was published. He was a leading churchman who denounced the theory of demons and Satan. His book also included a comprehensive account of all the methods of dowsing that were in use at the time. Abbé de Vallemont thought dowsing worked by an exchange of invisible corpuscles, both from the dowser to the rod, and from the object being searched for. His book includes an illustration of a dowser holding the traditional forked twig, with smoke rising from the ground to indicate the exchange of corpuscles.

Thomas de Quincey talks favorably about dowsing in his 1822 book, *The Confessions of an English Opium-eater.* He wrote:

> *In Somersetshire, which is a county the most ill-watered of all in England, upon building a house, there arises uniformly a difficulty in selecting a proper spot for a well. The remedy is to call in a set of local rhabdomantists. These men traverse the adjacent ground, holding the willow wand horizontally: wherever that dips, or inclines itself spontaneously to the ground, there will be found water. I have myself not only seen the process tried with success, but have witnessed the enormous trouble, delay, and expense, accruing to those of the opposite faction who refused to benefit by this art.*[9]

It is interesting to note that even in the early nineteenth century many people were reluctant to use dowsers, even though it put them to extra expense. This reluctance is especially surprising, as many professional dowsers worked on a "No water, no payment" basis.[10] Dowsing was also recognized as an accredited trade and some dowsers took on pupils and taught the skill to others.

The most famous dowser of the nineteenth century was John Mullins, born in 1838. He discovered his dowsing ability by accident. In 1859, he was helping to build a large house on the Ashwick Estate in Gloucestershire. A dowser was brought in from Cornwall to find water for the property. This dowser located a line where water would be found, and Sir John Ould, owner of the estate, asked the people watching to try for themselves. Sir John's daughter tried the rod and the response was so great that she threw it away. A well was dug at the site and provided plenty of water. A few days later, Sir John Ould decided to test everyone working on the house, some one hundred and fifty people. When it was John Mullins' turn, the dowsing response was so strong that the rod snapped.

John Mullins thought the experience was interesting and enjoyed being dubbed a "dowser" by his workmates. However, it was not until Sir John asked him to locate water at a nearby farm that he started to take the subject seriously. His rod selected a spot, and water was found there eighty-five feet below the surface. The yield was two hundred gallons an hour. After this success, John Mullins became very popular as a dowser. All the same, he was cautious and kept on working as a mason until 1882. In that year, he set himself up in business as a water diviner and well-sinker.

Shortly before his death in 1894, John Mullins was called in to find water at Warnham Lodge in Sussex. Sir Henry Harben, the owner, was skeptical about dowsing and refused to consider it. He drilled two wells that failed to produce any water. He then used the latest scientific methods to try again, and this well had to be abandoned also, after more than one thousand pounds had been spent on it.

Finally, Sir Henry agreed to call in John Mullins. Still skeptical, he met Mullins at the railway station to prevent him from obtaining any local knowledge. The two of them walked around the estate and Mullins' rod suddenly reacted. He told Sir Henry that they were over a small underground stream and that they would find a small supply of water there. However, Mullins was not satisfied. He wanted a larger volume of water. He decided to try higher ground, and marked out two locations. Both were later proved correct. He then proceeded to find further sites across the road where there were cottages belonging to the estate.

Sir Henry Harben decided to test Mullins' dowsing ability by having wells drilled at every site. They all provided water. A geologist then visited the estate and in his report wrote that John Mullins' success was "supernatural."

Such was Mullins' confidence in his abilities that he was prepared to receive no payment for sinking a well if no water was found. By the time he died, he had located more than five thousand sources of water. His sons carried on his business after his death, but were not nearly as successful.

John Mullins was accustomed to skepticism and was constantly tested by people considering using him. One interesting example was recorded in the Proceedings of the Society for Psychical Research. The Honorable M. E. G. Finch Hatton, a member of parliament, took John Mullins across his kitchen garden. There was a buried water pipe under the grass, but Mullins' rod did not recognize it. Mr. Finch Hatton was puzzled until he remembered that John Mullins had told him that his rod did not work over stagnant water. He asked a servant to turn on the tap and took John Mullins over the same ground again. This time his rod reacted. Mr. Finch Hatton carefully marked the spot with a twig and asked Mullins if he would do it again blindfolded. Mullins replied, "Oh yes, if you don't lead me into a pond or anything of that sort." Mr. Finch Hatton promised, blindfolded Mullins, and brought him back to the garden by a different route. Mullins' rod located the spot with mathematical precision. Mr. Finch Hatton later said that Mullins initially paused one foot beyond the original marker, but then turned around and let his rod locate the exact position.[11]

One of his sons, H. W. Mullins, had an interesting experience some years after his father had died. John Mullins had been called in to find water for the Right Honorable H. Chaplin, and successfully found a source. He told Mr. Chaplin the path of the underground river and indicated a spot on the other side of a fence, which he claimed would be an excellent site for a well. A marker was placed on this site, but the well was not dug and the site was lost. Eight years later, H. W. Mullins was called in to try and locate the position his father had indicated as more water was required. Mr. Mullins located a spot, and as the well was being dug, the workers recovered the buried marker that had been used by his father. The well turned out to be an excellent source.[12]

In the late 1880s a fourteen-year-old boy, Fred Rodwell, achieved fame with his ability at hand dowsing. He clasped his hands together while dowsing. When he was standing over the item he was divining for, his hands would lock together with such force that he could not separate them until he moved away from the spot. Like many other dowsers of the past and present, he was subjected to a great deal of ridicule and skepticism. At one time he was tested by Sir Ray Lankester, a noted skeptic, who treated the lad very harshly. Fred Rodwell's father wrote a letter of complaint saying his son was almost "frightened to death."[13] It is amazing that Fred achieved even partial success when he was nervous and scared.

In the nineteenth century, there were many educated people who considered dowsing to be scientific. One of these was Professor Herbert Mayo, who had the Chair of Physiology at King's College, University of London. He wrote that very soon dowsing "will be a credit to the family of superstitions, for without any reduction, or slipping, or trimming, it may at once assume the rank of a new truth."[14]

The Society for Psychical Research conducted a great deal of research into dowsing, and in the second volume of their *Proceedings for 1884,* decided that dowsing was legitimate and should be studied further. However, it should be noted that not all of the membership agreed, and some regarded dowsers as charlatans.

Happily oblivious to the scientific research going on into dowsing at that time were many peasants who had the skill but no explanation for it.

One of these was Bill Stone, who worked at Bolingbrook Hall. He did not think that you needed a specific "temperament." He would talk cheerfully to others while walking around with his forked twig. He "didn't need to concentrate," he said, as he "just let the thing work himself." He thought it might work by a type of magnetism, as a doctor had told him that he had a lot of iron in his system. He considered his power "a good thing," particularly when he successfully found water on the estate, after his employers had paid one hundred pounds on a failed attempt using other methods.[15]

The skepticism of many is in striking contrast to the giant Swiss pharmaceutical company Hoffmann-La Roche. When asked why they always used dowsers when building new laboratories around the world, Dr. Peter Treadwell, their spokesman and chief dowser, replied: "We use methods that are profitable, whether they are scientifically explainable or not. The dowsing method pays off."[16] Dr. Treadwell has successfully found water in countries as far away from Europe as Australia and India. He uses a large aluminum hoop as a divining rod, finding this lightweight piece of equipment less tiring than other dowsing instruments. According to the company's in-house magazine, *Roche-Zeitung*, Hoffmann-La Roche has been 100 percent successful in finding water wherever it was needed.[17] Many other corporations have also employed dowsers to find water. These include RCA, Bristol-Myers and Canadian Industries, partly owned by the Du Pont organization.[18]

Even governments have been prepared to use them. In 1931, the government of British Columbia employed Miss Evelyn Penrose as an official dowser. She also did work for the British and Australian governments.[19] Major W. N. Pogson became official water-diviner to the government of India. During the three years he held this position, water was found in forty-seven out of forty-nine sites he located. From 1941 to 1946, Norah Millen was the executive dowser to the government of Ceylon.

The armed forces have made use of dowsers throughout history. The Australian Expeditionary Forces used dowsers to find water at Gallipoli during World War I. Sapper S. Kelley volunteered to find water when the British Expeditionary Force was nearing exhaustion due to intense heat and lack of water. Using a bent piece of copper band, he located a spring within one hundred yards of the Divisional headquarters. This spring provided 2,000 gallons of pure water an hour. In the following week, Sapper Kelley located thirty-two wells that produced enough water to give all 100,000 men a gallon of water every day. During the 1930s, the Italian army used dowsers to locate water during their Turkish campaign. General Patton used a water diviner to locate water in

Morocco, as the Germans had destroyed the existing wells. I have a friend who successfully dowsed with coat hangers bent into an L-shape during the Vietnam War. He was originally skeptical, but became a firm believer after trying it himself.

The October 13, 1967, *New York Times* had a headline: "Dowsers detect enemy's tunnels." This article described how the Marines used two coat hangers, each bent into an L-shape to detect hidden tunnels. Louis Matacia, a land surveyor and dowser, offered his services free of charge to the American military. After testing him, they finally sent him to Vietnam to teach his method to the Marines of the 2nd Battalion, 5th Marine Regiment. His methods were initially regarded with skepticism, as *The Observer*, a weekly newspaper for the U.S. forces in Vietnam, reported in their March 13, 1967, issue. However, "Matacia's Wire Rudder," as the Marines called it, worked. *The Observer* article reported the success of Private Don R. Steiner the very first time he used them. The rods moved apart as he passed a Vietnamese hut. Inside the building the Marines discovered a tunnel that led to a family bunker directly beneath where Steiner had been standing when the rods reacted.

The Royal School of Military Engineering in Chatham, England, has perhaps the world's largest collection of material on dowsing, and they occasionally provide demonstrations for visiting skeptics. These unofficial tests are invariably successful, but the school has had little success in proving the reality of dowsing in organized scientific tests.

Despite this, a Royal Engineer was responsible for one of the most significant dowsing successes in recent times. In 1952, Colonel Harry Grattan, CBE, was responsible for building a new headquarters for the British Army in Mönchen Gladbach, Germany. The headquarters would ultimately house at least nine thousand people, which meant that Colonel Grattan had to find at least three-quarters of a million gallons of water a day. Unfortunately, water was in short supply. The Germans were using water that was alkaline and hard, and it would have been very expensive for the British to purchase. Colonel Grattan was aware that a wealthy family in the area was obtaining much softer water from their own well.

The Colonel began by obtaining advice from geologists and drilling a few trial wells, which produced nothing. Despite his engineering training, Colonel Grattan had experimented with dowsing in the past and decided to try again. He discovered he could dowse on horseback or while driving a car, just as easily as he could on foot. He gradually mapped out thirty square miles of countryside containing pure, soft water. The bores drilled into this area provided more than a million gallons of water a day, and are still doing this more than forty years later.[20]

The Soviet army has also used dowsers and even conducted classes on the subject for up to two hundred soldiers at a time.[21]

Dowsers have proven to be just as useful once the war is over. Abbé Bouly was able to locate buried shells after World War I and restore huge areas of war-ravaged land to cultivation. Incidentally, he was also able to determine which shells were German and which ones belonged to the Allies.

Unfortunately, the lack of success dowsers have in scientific tests has lead to a great deal of skepticism. Tom Graves hypothesizes that dowsing works when there is a "need" to be successful. This "need" is not present in scientific tests.

Actually, not all of the controlled tests have been failures. In his autobiography published in 1798, Arthur Young reported a test performed by Sir Joseph Banks on Captain Hoar, a celebrated dowser. Although Banks thought that Hoar had failed in one of the tests, Young wrote: "In the four trials I watched, and in which I knew he could not be acquainted with the direction of the pipes, he succeeded completely."

A more conclusive test of dowsing was conducted by Armand Viré, a French biologist, in 1913. Viré had a laboratory in the catacombs beneath Paris where he conducted experiments on animals that lived underground. Initially, he was a total skeptic. In his book he wrote: "Anything that related to dowsing seemed wholly cockeyed and unjustifiable to me."[22]

Henri Mager, a geographer, asked him to set up some tests for the Second Congress on Experimental Psychology. Mager explained that it was expensive to drill for water, but Viré could easily arrange tests using his knowledge of the underground caverns. For some 2,000 years, a huge network of underground quarries had been dug under Paris. Viré agreed.

He asked the dowsers to be outside the Daumesnil Gate at 8 A.M. the following Thursday. The area he had in mind consisted of a large lawn, divided by macadamized roads. There was no indication of the excavations sixteen to twenty meters below.

To Viré's immense surprise, all of the dowsers were successful. They all told him the correct depth of the excavations. Monsieur Probst indicated sixteen points on the ground to mark out three squares and a rectangle. He was even able to indicate the columns that had been put in place to prevent cave-ins.

Abbé Alexis Mermet confounded him even further. Not only did he point out all the tunnels and spaces that Viré knew about, but he also indicated one that had been unknown to anyone. Mermet was also tested on his ability to determine when water was flowing through a pipe nine meters below the ground. Mermet was able to tell instantly when water started to flow, but was just a fraction late in determining when it was turned off again. Viré was again impressed, realizing that a small amount of water continued to flow for a while after the tap was turned off.

Viré, forced to admit that dowsing was real, began to study more deeply and became an excellent advocate for the subject. He also became a good dowser himself.

Incidentally, at this same Congress, Joseph Mathieu asked to be tested for something that no one had heard of until then. He claimed to be able to dowse for water using a map and a pendulum. He successfully passed the test, and became the first map dowser on record.

Throughout history there have been many eminent men and women who were successful dowsers.

Leonardo da Vinci, Robert Boyle, Sir Isaac Newton, Lloyd George, Thomas A. Edison, and Dr. Albert Einstein are just a few.

Perhaps because it has always been part of European life, dowsing is more accepted there. Certainly the scientists are less skeptical. A 1953 UNESCO study of radiesthesia conducted by leading European scientists came to the conclusion that there was "no doubt that it (dowsing) is a fact." The Institute of Technical Physics of the Dutch National Research Council has endorsed dowsing, and the Academie des Sciences in France declared that "it is impossible to deny the existence of the power, although its nature cannot be determined."[23]

The argument still goes on, with learned people on both sides of the fence. Some excellent books and articles on the subject have been written by skeptics,[24] but unfortunately there have also been many produced by people who are not prepared to suspend disbelief long enough to give dowsing a fair trial.

CHAPTER ONE

The Tools

Fortunately, very little equipment is necessary for dowsing and most of it you can make yourself very easily. Years ago, I made myself a pair of angle rods from two coat hangers. They work just as well as an expensive set I later bought, which contain ball bearings to ensure smooth movement.

ANGLE RODS

Angle rods are the best tools to start with (See Figure 1A) as almost everyone is able to make them work. They consist of two L-shaped pieces of metal wire.

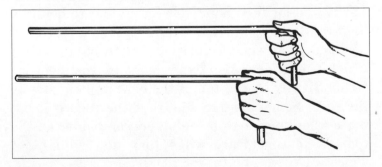

Figure 1A: Angle Rods

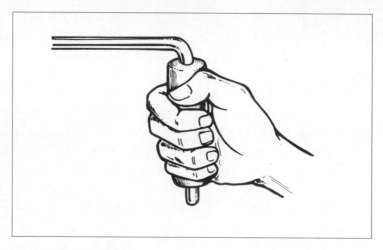

Figure 1B: Rod Covers

Mine have a twelve-inch long section that faces forward and a six-inch section that is held loosely in the hands. The measurements are not important as long as you feel comfortable holding them.

Most dowsers cover the shorter section with plastic or wood tubing (See Figure 1B). This allows the rods to swing freely no matter how tightly the dowser is gripping them. The shell of a ball-point pen works well for this. Some dowsers prefer to hold the bare rods loosely in their hands. This is a matter of personal preference. Experiment with both and see which you prefer. Also experiment by resting your thumb lightly on the top of the bend to help steady the rods. Some dowsers find that the rods will not move when they do this, but others complain that the rods move constantly when they don't. Find out which way works better for you.

The rods are held in the hands with the longer sections parallel and pointing straight ahead. When the dowser locates whatever it is he or she is searching for the rods will either cross over each other, or move outward. This is called a "dowsing response."

Some dowsers use just one angle rod and know when they are over the correct location by a ninety degree movement of the rod. Soldiers in Vietnam used a single rod, as they carried a rifle in their other hand. They successfully dowsed for underground tunnels, ammunition dumps, traps, and buried mines.

Divining Rods

These are the traditional forked sticks which are V- or Y-shaped pieces of branch cut from a tree (See Figure 1C). Usually, they are cut from hazel, apple, peach, cherry, willow, or birch trees. Other trees can be used, but these retain their flexibility far longer than others. In the United States, the

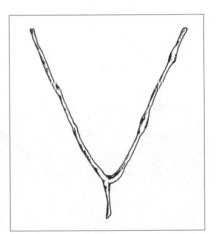

Figure 1C: Divining Rod

peach and the willow seem to be the most popular trees for making divining rods. I personally prefer the apple. Many diviners cut a new rod every time they need one, as the wood quickly dries out and becomes brittle. It is important for the rod to be supple.

One of the reasons dowsing used to be considered a special gift is because, in the past, one-inch thick rods were often used. Not surprisingly, very few people were able to use them, as they were heavy and hard to handle.

The two arms of the rod are usually about eighteen inches long and have an inside angle of between forty to seventy degrees. This is a matter of personal preference and you will have to experiment with longer and shorter arms and different angles to find one that feels just right for you. If you use rods with extremely long arms, your own hands and arms will tire more quickly.

Divining rods do not need to be cut from wood. In the early part of this century they were often made from whalebone. Nowadays, plastic and fiberglass are popular. You can easily make your own by binding two pieces of plastic tubing together. If you use circular tubing, shave down the sections that touch each other to make a smooth join. I use white plastic so that I can easily find my rod again if I place it down somewhere. Rods made from green, brown, or black plastic can be hard to locate if placed down in the middle of a large open space when you are dowsing.

A friend who belongs to the same dowsing society as I do makes her own V-shaped rods from two knitting needles and a large cork. She sticks the pointed ends of the knitting needles into the cork, fastens them in place with adhesive tape, and is ready to dowse. This makes an extremely flexible, and sensitive, dowsing instrument.

Hold the rod with your palms upward and grip the rod in such a way as to bend the forks out. Keep your elbows close to your sides. When you walk over whatever it is you are divining for, the rod will— usually—turn downward with a very strong pull. Occasionally, it will turn upward. Several of my students have been hit on the head with their rods.

THE PENDULUM

The pendulum consists of a weight attached to a length of cord or chain (See Figure 1D). Ideally, the weight should be at least a few ounces. However, it also should not be so heavy that your hand gets tired quickly. Major General J. Scott Elliot (author of *Dowsing One Man's Way*) began by using an extremely light pendulum—a Christmas tree ornament. I have used a paperclip attached to a length of thread when nothing else was available, and it worked very well. All the same, I feel more comfortable with a heavier weight.

Almost anything that can be suspended on a length of thread or chain will do. Over the years I have built up a rather eclectic collection of pendulums. These range from the chain pull of a light fitting to a miniature Tibetan dagger, and even to a plastic skull. People often give me pendants and novelty items that they think I would enjoy using as pendulums, so my collection is growing all the time. I

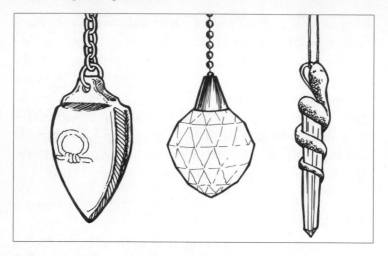

Figure 1D: Different Types of Pendulums

would not choose most of these for serious dowsing work, but would have no hesitation in using them when nothing else is available. Some authorities[1] claim that the pendulum should be made of wood or any other substance that does not conduct electricity. I have not found this to be the case myself, and have a number of pendulums made from different metals that work very well.

My favorite pendulum is a Mermet pendulum, designed by the famous French radiesthesist, Abbé Mermet. He had some astonishing successes in the early part of this century, and his books are still essential reading.

The Mermet pendulum can be unscrewed and a small sample of whatever is being dowsed for is placed inside. The pendulum is suspended from the thumb and first finger and the different movements it makes are interpreted. Mermet pendulums are available at many New Age bookstores.

The Wand

The wand was originally a three-foot-long piece of thin, tapered, springy wood (See Figure 1E). Nowadays, it is more common for a length of plastic or nylon to be used. The wand is held at the thinner end, and the diviner walks with the thick end suspended a few inches above the ground. When the end of the stick is over the object being divined for, the stick starts to bob up and down. This is why it is frequently known as a bobbing stick.

It is believed that the more familiar Y-shaped divining rod is descended from the bobbing stick. This is because early pictures of dowsers in operation usually show them holding a straight rod that has been partially split to enable them to hold it easily in both hands.

The wand is usually used nowadays to determine the depth of the item being sought under the ground. Each up-and-down movement (or bob) represents a unit of measurement, usually ten feet. When the wand stops bobbing and starts moving from side to side, it is an indication that you have determined the depth.

Figure 1E: The Wand

OTHER TYPES OF RODS

Almost anything can, and probably has been, used for dowsing. Over the years many people have come up with different ideas and some of these have been manufactured and marketed. Probably the best known of these is the Aurameter, which was invented by Verne Cameron. It contains a spring designed to make the rod more sensitive.[2] Nowadays, many people are using semi-circular hoops made of a light material, such as aluminum. Thin branches can also be flexed into a semi-circle and used for dowsing. It is possible that this is one of the earliest known dowsing devices.

OTHER DEVICES

Over the years I have seen a wide range of objects used for dowsing purposes. Pliers, particularly the slip-jointed ones, work well. So do scissors. Some people use metal coat hangers in their original shape. They are held by the corners of the long side with the handle in front. The movements of this handle provide the dowsing response. I have also seen a man dowsing for water with a twelve inch wooden ruler. He held one end in each hand. When he was standing over a water source his hands twisted downwards, breaking the ruler. He told me that this was not his normal method, but nothing else was available at the time.

Many years ago at a dowsing society meeting, I saw a man dowsing with a pencil. He held it in his right hand as if he were going to write with it, but his fingers were in position at the blunt end, rather than the writing end. He simply stared at the tip of the pencil and asked it questions. The pencil indicated the answers with a jerky movement.

HAND DOWSING

Some dowsers do not need the help of rods or pendulums. They dowse with their hands. They walk over the area being searched while shaking their hands. Consequently, they are often referred to as "hand tremblers." Their hands suddenly stop shaking when they are standing over the object they are divining for. Hand dowsing is very rare. The reason for this is that most dowsers need some sort of device to channel the information from the subconscious mind.

Different hand dowsers experience varying types of dowsing responses. Some experience a feeling of heat in the hands, others a sensation of cold. Some experience the hairs on their arms rising and others an itchy feeling in the palms of their hands. A friend of mine experiences a tingling sensation in his fingers.

Another common form of hand dowsing is simply extending both arms straight out in front of you, parallel to the ground. The arms should be rigid. When you are over your target one arm will start to rise. With some people, the shoulder also rises.

As it is very tiring keeping the muscles rigid in this way, some dowsers extend just one arm. When it gets tired, they extend the other arm.

Leicester Gataker was a successful hand dowser in England in the late Victorian era. His method was to walk rapidly over the area being surveyed with his hands by his sides. Eyewitnesses said he became instantly agitated as soon as he felt he was in the vicinity of water. He would then outstretch his hands and apparently feel the exact area to drill. His hands would also tell him the depth and volume of water. He said that he felt a tingling sensation throughout his entire body when he was standing over water.[3]

Hand dowsers have a variety of ways of holding their hands. Raymond Willey, a former secretary of the American Society of Dowsers and author of *Modern Dowsing*, worked with his hands held in fists with the thumbs pointing towards his body. The balls of the thumbs were tightly pressed together at an angle of ninety degrees. When he reached his target, his thumbs would instantly point downwards, and the ninety degree angle would change to a straight line.[4]

I have also seen people dowsing with their forefingers pressed together. In this variation, the hands are formed into fists with the forefingers extended away from the person. The forefingers are pressed together, making an angle of between one hundred and one hundred and twenty degrees. Finally, the hands are held straight out from the body at about forehead height. The forefingers act just like dowsing rods when over the desired object. I have also seen a lady dowsing in this way using the little finger of each hand.

Another method is clasping the two hands together with the forefingers extended. The tips of the forefingers are gently touching each other. When the dowser is in the vicinity of the item he or she is dowsing for, the forefingers press tightly together and cannot be separated until the dowser moves away.

Another method is for the dowser to rub the thumb and forefinger together until it feels rough. Some people describe the sensation as "feeling sticky."

Uri Geller, by far the most financially successful dowser of all time, dowses with his hands.

Raymond Willey also described a man who could dowse with his feet. He would walk over the area being dowsed, with his question in mind. When he was standing directly over a vein of water, he would feel the response in the muscles in the small of his back.[5]

You should experiment with hand dowsing, as it can be very useful when nothing else is available. It also means that you can dowse anywhere at any time.

BODY DOWSING

Some dowsers use their entire bodies as a dowsing instrument. They may sway from side to side. They might experience muscular tension or a tic in certain parts of their bodies.

In the eighteenth century, Daniel Wilson, a clergyman, discovered that he started blinking over underground water. He was also able to use this blinking talent to answer questions.[6]

This covers the main tools that dowsers use. You should try as many of them as possible to find the tools that are best for you. Probably the easiest method to start with is the angle rods. Almost everyone finds hand dowsing the most difficult, but I have met a number of people who have never used any other method. Most dowsers nowadays use the pendulum as their preferred method.

CHAPTER TWO

Using the Tools

ANGLE RODS

Angle rods are easily made from two wire coat hangers (See Figure 2A). This is how my first ones were made some twenty-five years ago, and I am still using them. Once you have cut two pieces of wire, bend each into a right angle to make an L shape. The shorter side should be about six inches long and the longer side between twelve and twenty inches. Slide the short sides into plastic straws, and you are ready to start.

Hold the angle rods loosely in your fists with the long section of the wire pointing straight ahead. Your hands should be approximately body-width apart. Do not tuck your elbows into your sides. The rods should be parallel to each other. This is known as the "neutral" position. If your angle rods are encased in a tube of plastic or wooden dowel, you can grasp this outer casing as firmly as you wish, as the rods can move independently inside it. However, if you are not using a casing, you must hold the rods very loosely, so that they can give a dowsing response.

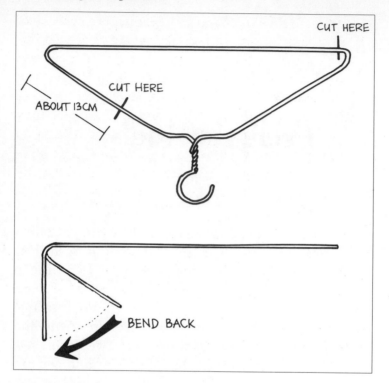

Figure 2A: Making Angle Rods from a Hanger

For example, my friend, Brian Reid, holds his angle rods with his thumb and first two fingers. The rods go outside his third and fourth fingers. He does not use a casing.

Once you have experienced a dowsing response with your angle rods, try holding them in different ways and see which you prefer. There is no right or wrong way of holding any dowsing instrument.

Now go for a walk and see if you can maintain the rods in the neutral position. I started by practicing indoors rather than out in the open where other people could see me. It is probably better to do this initial practicing on your own, so you may wish to start indoors as well. Keep as relaxed as possible, and keep your eyes on the tips of the rods as you walk.

Stop and rest after a few minutes. Your rods may have moved at times as you walked. You will have to determine if this was caused by inadvertent movements of your hands, or if the rods were moving by themselves, indicating a dowsing response.

It is highly likely that the rods did not move at all. This does not matter. You have gained some experience at walking with your rods in a neutral position without accidentally making them move.

After you are comfortable with this, it is time to go outdoors to experiment further. Choose a windless day for this, as wind can cause the rods to move and make dowsing more difficult. This time we will dowse for something specific. The best thing to start

THE AUTHOR
DEMONSTRATES USING
ANGLE RODS.

with is water, so try to dowse for the water pipe that brings water to your home. It does not matter if you already know approximately where this pipe is. The rods will tell you the exact location.

Before you start, take a few deep breaths and tell yourself that you are going to dowse for the water pipe. Keep thinking about the water pipe while you do the following exercise. Be confident and receptive, but do not try too hard. I find an open-minded approach, along with a positive expectancy that I will locate water, yield the best results for me.

Start by walking from one side of the property to the other with your rods in the neutral position. At some stage the rods will probably move across each other. As you get close to the source of water the rods will start to move towards each other and finally cross when they are right over the water (See Figure 2B). Frequently, they will keep on crossing until they are parallel to each other in front of your chest. Make a note of where on the property this position occurred. Go across the property again about a yard away from where you walked before. The rods will doubtless cross each other again at about the same place.

It is likely that your rods will cross each other just after you cross the water mains. For some reason, most beginners overreach the source of water. With practice, you will find that they will cross when you are exactly on top of the source.

Your initial practice session should be short, perhaps twenty or thirty minutes. Dowsing can be draining, both physically and mentally. Not only

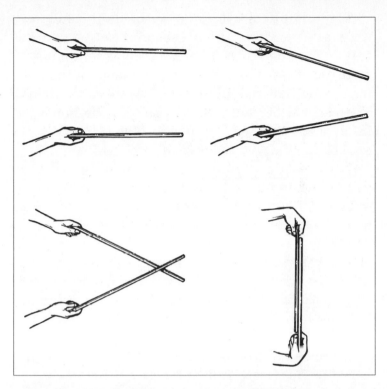

Figure 2B: Angle Rods Showing a Crossing Response

does it require great concentration, but it also keeps certain muscles under constant tension. Because of this, once you get tired your results will be contradictory. Even now, after more than a quarter of a century of dowsing, I pause and rest every now and again to try to avoid mistakes caused by fatigue.

Many people find that the rods move the very first time they attempt to dowse. Others need to practice a bit first.

If you fail to detect any movements in your rods, try walking along the street and see if you get results from detecting other people's water mains.

If you still fail to have any movements in the rods, make sure that you are not holding them too tightly. They should be held either loosely in the hands, or inside a sleeve of wood or plastic. Make sure that you are holding the rods as horizontal as possible.

Long rods give an extremely clear reaction, so you might find it helpful to experiment with rods of different lengths. Unfortunately, longer rods are more tiring to use. I know an elderly couple who dowse successfully with angle rods. Hers are tiny, about two inches by three inches. His, on the other hand, are immense, some six inches by thirty inches. It looks rather comical when they are out dowsing together. However, he needs to stop and rest frequently, while she can go on indefinitely.

Dowsers are usually able to divine moving water. Very few can locate still water. If you are having no success in locating your water pipes, try turning a faucet on for a couple of minutes to get the water flowing.

The other possibility is that there is no water pipe in the area you have been dowsing. Naturally, if there is no water to be found, the rods will not move.

Finally, if your rods will not move no matter where you go, find an experienced dowser. Ask this person to place a hand on your shoulder or wrist as you dowse. Somehow, this action will enable your rods to move and you will have no difficulty after that in getting the right reaction.

**THE AUTHOR
SHOWING A CROSSING
RESPONSE WITH
ANGLE RODS.**

It is very helpful to spend time with an experienced dowser. You will find they are all enthusiastic about dowsing and are usually happy to help beginners. Most are sharing people. You will learn more from a few hours dowsing alongside someone like this than you will absorb from a dozen books on the subject. See if there is a dowsing society in your area. Most large cities have one, and you will learn a great deal by spending time in the company of like-minded people.

Experiment with your rods in different locations. Try, whenever possible, to dowse for water in places that you can verify afterwards. Sewers, drains, and even underground streams are all good examples. Close to where I live is a park with an underground stream that meanders diagonally across it. This makes an excellent place to practice dowsing.

Being able to dowse for water is a very useful and practical skill. A couple of years ago, the pipe bringing water to our house burst. As this water main was underneath a long concrete drive the repairmen would have had to dig it all up to find where the pipe had burst. This would have been a very lengthy and expensive task. All I had to do was walk up the path with my rods, asking them to tell me where the pipe had burst. I was then able to tell the plumbers exactly where to dig and the pipe was repaired for a fraction of the estimated cost we had been given. This is just one of a number of occasions where dowsing has saved me both time and money.

After experimenting with the angle rods, you will become aware that it is your hands that are making the rods move. Tiny, subconscious movements that you probably could not discern without the rods cause this to happen. This, of course, is why some people are able to dowse successfully with nothing but their hands. The angle rods are simply a tool to amplify these small movements.

Once you can use angle rods, you will be able to find your way anywhere in the world. Hold one angle rod and ask it to indicate north. You will find it will move until the pointer is facing north. Check the accuracy with a compass to confirm what the angle rod is indicating. Now, ask it to find east and it will move ninety degrees until it is facing due east. This is a useful test which I frequently use when discussing dowsing with open-minded people.

THE Y-SHAPED ROD

The Y- or V-shaped dowsing rod can be made from almost anything, but I suggest you start with a forked branch cut from a tree (See Figure 2C). Most dowsers prefer a newly-cut branch, as it is much more supple than dryer wood. In the past there was a great deal of ritual attached to choosing the right branch. For instance, the branch

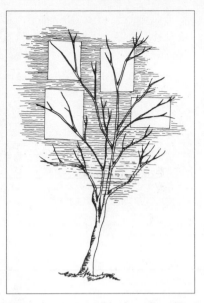

Figure 2C: Parts of a Tree from Which to Cut a Y-shaped Rod

was selected in the evening and then cut the following morning.

You do not need to concern yourself with anything like that. Choose a suitable branch and cut it with a pruning shear. The two arms should be between eighteen and twenty-four inches long, and the pointer somewhere between two and four inches long. Trim off any side branches, so that you are left with a Y-shaped dowsing rod.

There are two ways of holding the rod. The more usual one is to grasp the forks near the ends with your hands held palms upwards (See Figure 2D). I like to have about an inch of the fork protruding

**THE AUTHOR FINDS AN
APPROPRIATE BRANCH
FOR A ROD.**

**WHEN TRIMMED
THE BRANCH MAKES
A SUITABLE
Y-SHAPED ROD.**

from my hands. Many diviners rest their thumbs on, or over, this protruding portion. You will feel a certain amount of tension between your hands and the forks. Increase this tension to bend the forks slightly outwards. This is why we use a supple twig, of course, as a brittle one would break under the pressure. Stand with your elbows close to your sides and the rod pointing very slightly

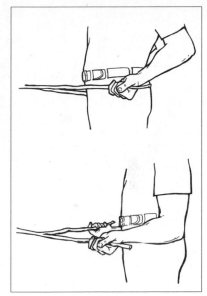

Figure 2D: Two Different Ways to Hold the Rod

upwards. Your upper arms and forearms should create an angle of between eighty and ninety degrees.

Holding the dowsing rod in this way puts stress on the rod. Consequently, when you are standing over the object you are searching for, the pull of the rod can be extremely strong. On many occasions I have found the pull to be so strong that the bark on the branch has been shredded from beneath my hands.

Some dowsers prefer to hold the rod closer to their bodies and have their fists touching their hips. I prefer to hold the rod with my elbows touching my sides. Experiment with both positions and see which one feels more natural for you.

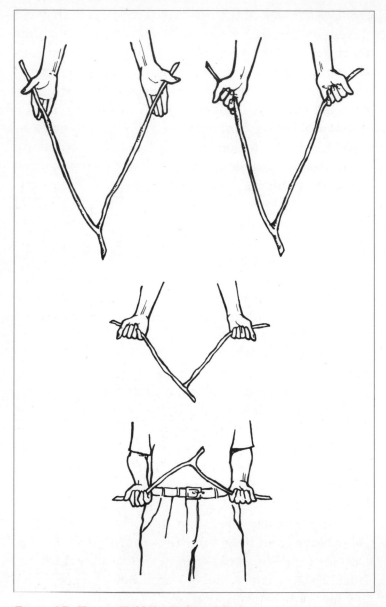

Figure 2E: How to Hold the Y-shaped Rod

Another way of holding the rod is with your hands held palm downward. This is not nearly as common as the palms-upward method, and is usually performed with older, less flexible branches. Hold the forks with your fingers and have your thumbs pointing towards the joint, putting compression on the wood. The rod should be pointing upwards at about a forty-five degree angle. The dowsing response is very marked, and is a strong pull inwards towards the body and down. Many people also experience a slight up-and-down movement of the stick, almost as if the stick has a life of its own and is enthusiastically hunting for the object of the search.

I can make the rod work holding it either way, but find I get more tension in the wood, and consequently a much better movement, with my palms

THE AUTHOR
HOLDS THE ROD IN
A PALMS DOWN
POSITION.

upward. Again, experiment and see which way works better for you. You may want to try holding the rod in a variety of different ways to see if you get a better response.

John Mullins, the celebrated nineteenth century dowser, always held his rod with the first and second fingers of each hand. The back of the third and fourth fingers rested on the two branches of the rod. Other dowsers have been recorded using other methods. William Stokes, another Victorian diviner, grasped the two branches of the rod in his fists with the rod pointing to the ground.[1]

Again, try holding the branch in both the palms-up and palms-down position, and practice walking with it. When you feel you are ready, start thinking about water and walk slowly. Maintain a feeling of positive expectancy. You may feel a few faint tugs or twists as you approach a water source, followed by the major pull. However, do not be disturbed if this does not happen. Many people feel nothing until the branch suddenly moves strongly.

Usually, the rod is pulled strongly downward when the stick is held in the palms-upward position. You will feel as if the tip of the rod is being pulled toward the ground. However, with some people, the movement is upward. You will not know which way it will move for you until you try for yourself. Some years ago, I watched a husband and wife dowsing together. The husband's rod was pulled downwards, and at the same moment his wife's rod went upwards. I have since seen two other couples who

Figure 2F: Getting a Dowsing Response

A DOWNWARD RESPONSE PULLS
THE AUTHOR'S ROD SHARPLY
TOWARD THE GROUND.

also have the opposite dowsing response to each
other.

If you have already practiced with the angle rods
try going over the same areas with a dowsing rod to
see what happens. You may find you have a preference for one instrument over the other.

THE PENDULUM

The angle rods and Y-shaped rod are usually used
out-of-doors. The pendulum is normally used for

indoor dowsing. However, all of them can be used in or out-of-doors if required.

The pendulum is simply a small object suspended on a length of thread or chain. Many dowsers prefer wooden pendulums, just as many prefer to work with wooden Y-shaped rods rather than plastic ones. However, you may prefer to have a crystal or metal pendulum. Some dowsers do not like metal pendulums as they claim that they pick up vibrations from similar metals in the soil. I have not found that to be the case. Abbé Mermet designed a special metal pendulum, made from an alloy of several metals, and this is what I normally use. New Age bookstores often have attractive displays of pendulums and you can choose one that appeals to you. My Mermet pendulum came from a New Age store. The plumb-bobs used by carpenters are actually pendulums, and dowsers often refer to their pendulums as "bobs."

If you buy a pendulum, rather than make one yourself, you will have to eliminate the energies the pendulum will have picked up from the people who handled it before it came into your possession. If it is made of crystal or metal, you will be able to wash it. With a wooden bob you can eliminate the old energies and attune it to your vibrations by rubbing it briskly between your hands.

For dowsing purposes, the length of the string need not be very long. Start with just half an inch of thread, with the rest held in the palm of your hand. Hold the pendulum so that the cord is gripped between your thumb and first finger and your fingers are pointing downwards. Swing the pendulum back and forth. Slowly release more and more thread until the pendulum starts to revolve in circles.

Make a knot at the center of the thread that is below your finger and thumb. This is the correct spot to hold the pendulum when you are dowsing with it.

Now you are ready to ask your pendulum some questions. Hold it at the knot you just tied and ask it to tell you which movement means "yes."

Be patient. The pendulum may take a while, but eventually it will start to move and give you the answer. My pendulum gyrates in a clockwise direction for "yes." Your pendulum may make a completely different movement. It may oscillate from side to side, or go around in circles, either clockwise or counter-clockwise. Remember the movement for "yes," and then ask it to tell you what movement indicates "no." My pendulum moves backwards and forwards for "no." Your pendulum may do something completely different. This is exactly the same as the old tradition of using a wedding ring suspended on a string to determine the sex of an unborn child. One type of movement indicates a boy and another a girl.

You can now ask your pendulum any questions that can be answered by either "yes" or "no." Start by asking it about things you already know. You might ask, "Is my name...?" "Am I married...?" and so on. Once your pendulum has successfully answered simple questions like these, you can start asking it questions that you do not know the answer to. Be careful when asking questions for yourself, as the pendulum is likely to give you the answer that you want to hear, rather than the correct answer. If it is important that you have an answer, find someone else who is not emotionally involved to ask the question for you.

You will need to ask your pendulum regularly which movement is positive and which negative, as the movements can change, even from day to day. This may or may not happen with you. You may find that your initial movements remain constant forever. On the other hand, you may find it changes every single time you use your pendulum. It pays to confirm the pendulum's response every now and again.

THE WAND

The wand is an approximately three-foot-long piece of wood, wider at one end than the other. Some people use wands as short as two feet, and others use wands that are more than four feet long. The ideal wand is one that can be held horizontally at the narrow end, with the other end sagging no more than three inches. Select a suitable piece of wood and cut off any side branches with pruning shears. You can use it right away, if you are planning to discard it afterwards. If you intend to keep it for some time, it pays to put it aside for a few weeks to dry out.

Wands can be made out of almost anything. An extendible car antenna works very well, and has the advantage that it can be carried in a pocket when not being used. A friend of mine uses a broom handle. I find it too heavy to use for long, and much prefer a wand that is thinner at one end than the other.

Hold the thin end with both hands touching, one in front of the other, and allow the thick end to almost touch the ground in front of you.

You can dowse with this in the normal way. Decide what it is you are dowsing for, fix that in your mind, and then start walking slowly.

In practice, the wand is usually used for determining depth, after another device has located the desired item. The wand bobs up and down over the item and these can be read.

First of all, decide how many feet are indicated by each bob. You may decide that each bob represents ten feet. Next, ask the wand how many feet deep the item is, and count the number of bobs the wand makes. In this instance, if the wand bobs ten times, we know that the item is situated approximately one hundred feet down. (Each bob represents ten feet times ten bobs.) We can then alter the reading of the bobs so that each bob indicates, say, one foot. If the wand then bobs four more times, we know that the item is located one hundred and four feet below the surface.

CHAPTER THREE

More Advanced Dowsing

By now you should have experimented with angle rods, the V- or Y-shaped dowsing rod, and the pendulum. You will have developed a feel for them and be comfortable when using them.

You may have developed a preference for one method over another. This is natural. Peter Underwood tells of two eminent dowsers, a Mr. and Mrs. W N. Pogson, who originally used the Y-shaped rod exclusively, but changed to the angle rods when they discovered that the rods worked better for them.[1] I have a friend who has done exactly the opposite. He began with the angle rods and switched to a dowsing rod.

Try dowsing with other people, if possible. It is great fun, stimulates interest, and gives you an opportunity to practice with like-minded people. Choose your dowsing companions carefully. I enjoy dowsing with others, but loathe dowsing with people who want to talk all of the time. It is very hard to concentrate if someone else is chatting incessantly.

For almost twenty years, the leaders of Swampscott, Massachusetts, searched for a good water source to replace the supply they had lost. They received plenty of expert advice and used all of the most modern techniques. Nothing worked. After twenty years of being rationed every summer, the residents had had enough. At a meeting someone suggested dowsing. Mr. Paul A. Polisson, the Superintendent of Public Works, was skeptical, but at this stage he was prepared to try anything.

A group of volunteers started dowsing in a group. Just fifteen minutes after they started, a local laborer, "Dutchy" Emery, found a replacement water supply with a dowsing response so strong that it scraped skin off his thumb. Mr. Emery was a complete amateur who had never held a dowsing rod before.[2]

DOWSING SMALL AREAS

If you are dowsing for something in a small area, the easiest way is to simply walk from side to side in a zigzag fashion, starting in one corner (See Figure 3A). Think about the object you are searching for. Each time your rod gives a dowsing response, place a peg in the ground at that spot. In this way, you will gradually mark out the course of the waterpipe, or whatever else it is you are seeking.

DOWSING LARGER AREAS

It is possible to dowse larger areas by simply walking over them in a zigzag fashion, but this is time consuming, and often impractical, especially if you have hundreds of acres to dowse.

With larger areas, a pendulum is very useful in telling you where to begin. Stand on the edge of the area you will be dowsing. Hold your pendulum in your right hand (left if you are left-handed) and extend your other hand out in front of you with the fingers touching and the palm downwards.

Think about the item you are searching for. If it is water, ask yourself, "Where is the best supply of usable water to be found?" If you want drinking water, make sure to specify that in your question. It is important to be as specific as you can in asking these questions. Slowly move your left hand across

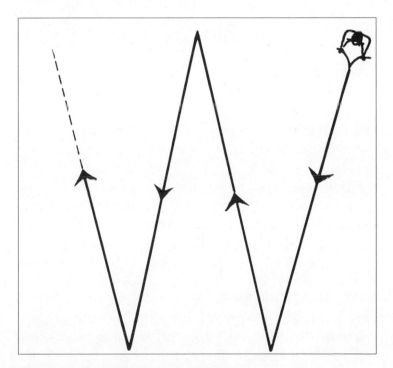

Figure 3A: Dowsing in a Zig-zag Pattern

HOLD THE ROD IN A POSITION THAT IS COMFORTABLE AS YOU START TO DOWSE. THE AUTHOR HOLDS THE ROD PALMS UPWARD.

the target area. When your hand is pointing in the right direction your pendulum will start to gyrate.

The Y-shaped rod also works well for this. Ask yourself the same question and slowly move in a semi-circle. When the rod is pointing in the right direction, it will dip sharply downwards.

You now know which direction the water is in. Now you can ask your pendulum, or your rod, "How far away is the water vein?" Start counting in units that are appropriate to the size of the area. You may count, "Ten feet? Twenty feet? Thirty feet?" until you get a response. The pendulum or rod will react when you get to the correct distance.

Once it has given you a positive distance, walk in the correct direction. Use your dowsing rod as you approach and mark the spot it indicates with a peg.

You will probably want to know the course of the water vein. You do this by moving thirty feet away and walking in a circle around the peg. Your rod will react twice. Place a peg at each location and you will have a good idea of the water's course. You can repeat this with wider and wider circles if you need greater accuracy.

How Far Down is the Water?

Congratulations! You have found a vein of usable water. We now need a method to tell us how deep the water is. Drilling is very expensive and if the depth is too great, it might be better to locate another source somewhere else on the property.

There are a number of methods for determining the depth. The one I use is to stand over the vein

THE ROD REACTS WITH A SHARP DOWNWARD MOVEMENT WHEN IT ANSWERS THE QUESTION OR FINDS THE CORRECT SPOT.

with my Y-shaped rod and ask it questions. "Tell me how far down the water vein is," I ask. "Is it ten feet? Is it twenty feet?" I keep on asking until my rod reacts. This will be at the ten foot distance nearest to the vein. I can now be more specific if I wish. Suppose my rod has reacted at one hundred and ten feet. I can now ask, "Is the water vein at one hundred and five feet? One hundred and six? One hundred and seven?" Somewhere between one hundred and five and one hundred and fifteen my rod will react and tell me the correct depth.

Marking Time Method

Another method is to stand over the position that your divining rod selected. Hold your rod and start marking time on the spot. Count each step you make. Each one represents one foot of depth. Your rod will give a dowsing response when you have reached the correct depth.

The Bishop's Rule

In eighteenth century France, the Bishop of Grenoble became fascinated with the talents of Barthelemy Bléton, a celebrated dowser. He conducted many tests and recorded Bléton's method of determining the depth of the vein.

Bléton would stand over the vein for a few moments before asking his rod to indicate the correct depth. He would then start walking away and his rod would react when he was as far away from the vein as

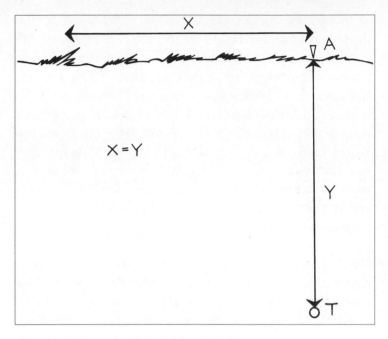

Figure 3B: Example of the Bishop's Rule

the depth of the water (See Figure 3B). He checked this measurement by walking in other directions to see if his rod reacted at the same distance each time.

The bishop recorded that this method was not always accurate, but it can be useful in confirming the findings of the previous methods.

WHAT IS THE YIELD?

We have found the water, and we know how far underground it is. Finally, we need to determine the yield of the vein. If the yield is small, it may not be worth the expense of drilling a well.

Again, we can determine this by using a rod or pendulum. Stand over the vein and ask, "How many gallons of water per minute will this vein provide? Ten gallons? Twenty gallons? Thirty gallons?" The divining instrument will react at the nearest ten gallons.

Lieutenant Colonel C. D. A. Fenwick recorded a different method of determining the yield of water, which he used in India. He would place a compass on the spot where he received a dowsing response and then walk around the site in circles until his divining rod reacted. Each full circle represented five hundred gallons of water per hour.[3]

A New Zealand dowser, seventy-year-old Brian Reid, uses a one-meter by three-millimeter rod to determine the yield of water. From past experience, he knows that if the rod moves from a horizontal position to a vertical one, 842,000 liters of water per hour will be found. At one location he divined recently, the rod reacted so strongly that it went over his shoulder and down his back. He then used a V-shaped dowsing rod which twisted around itself three times. A city council officer who was present kept the rod as a souvenir, saying that there was "no way could you bend it like that in your hands."

Mr. Reid had never experienced such a huge volume before. He asked Wanganui City Councilors if he could use one of their pumping stations to gauge the flow. At the pumping station he was told that the yield was 180,000 liters per hour. After testing with his dowsing rod Mr. Reid declared that the yield was only about 27,000 liters per hour. The Council officer was adamant that the flow was 180,000 liters per hour. After retesting, Mr. Reid was convinced that 27,000 liters per hour was the absolute maximum. The two men went into the pumping station and discovered that the pump had been turned off. The bore was free-flowing and was, in fact, around 27,000 liters per hour.[4]

OTHER QUESTIONS

It pays to ask as many questions as possible before going to the expense of drilling a well. You may have successfully located water, but will it be suitable for your needs? If you want drinking water, ask if the quality is good enough for this purpose. Your divining instrument will give you the correct answer.

Colonel K. W. Merrylees described one of his dowsing failures.[5] He had successfully dowsed for water, and also correctly gauged the depth and quantity. However, he neglected to ask about the quality. The well produced 22,000 gallons of water per hour, but it was too salty for agricultural use. He had neglected to ask about the quality as he had never come across water like that in England before.

Do not expect perfection at any of this initially. There are many dowsers who are experts at finding water, but cannot determine the depth or yield accurately. Practice and perseverance are necessary. The more you use your tools, and the more familiar you become with dowsing, the easier it will become.

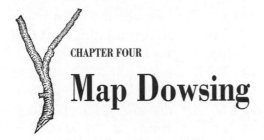

CHAPTER FOUR

Map Dowsing

Up until now, all of our dowsing has been done in the field. We have actually gone out and walked around with our equipment until we found whatever it was we were dowsing for.

Now we are going to take a great leap forward and experiment with map dowsing. There are many advantages to map dowsing. You can dowse for anything at all in any part of the world you choose, from the comfort of your own home. There are many recorded instances where map dowsing has been done from thousands of miles away.

Abbé Alexis Mermet was a celebrated dowser in France and Switzerland in the early part of this century. He specialized in healing with his pendulum, but was also extremely talented at finding missing people. He was also an extremely good water diviner and map-dowser. After World War I he used map-dowsing to locate the sites of German shells lying buried in French soil.

In 1927, he received a letter from Marist College in Colombia, South America, saying that the college would have to be closed due to a lack of water. They wanted Abbé Mermet to visit and dowse for water on the site. Abbé Mermet replied that he did not want to travel that far, but if they would send him a plan of the property, he would see what he could do.

When the map arrived, Mermet sat in his office at Saint-Prex, near Geneva, and dowsed it with his pendulum. He sent it back, with one site marked, telling them that they would find water at the spot at a depth of twenty-eight meters. The priests immediately drilled a well and found water at the exact depth that Mermet had specified. The rector wrote back, thanking Mermet, and asked if he would look at the plan again to see if there was any petroleum or metals to be found![1]

Abbé Mermet was recognized by the Vatican for his work in May 1935. This was an incredible accomplishment when one considers that most churches associated dowsing with witchcraft, and a few hundred years earlier Mermet would have been imprisoned or burned at the stake.

Another Frenchman, the Vicomte Henry de France, recorded some map dowsing successes achieved by a friend of his. Joseph Treyve was manager of a horticultural center in Moulins, France, and a keen dowser. Before he went out hunting for wild boar, he would invariably map dowse the area beforehand to find where the boar would be located.

One day, one of his workmen failed to report to work. Monsieur Treyve took out a street map of the city and suspended his pendulum over it. This told him exactly where his worker was drinking and

Monsieur Treyve was able to go to the café and order his employee back to work.[2]

In the 1940s, Henry Gross, quietly map dowsing at his home in Maine, successfully located the site of the first freshwater well in Bermuda. The historical novelist, Kenneth Roberts, wrote a book about him called *Henry Gross and His Dowsing Rod,* which became a bestseller in 1951.

In early 1959, Verne Cameron used his pendulum over a map of the Pacific Ocean and located the positions of all the submarines that were there at the time. He was also able to determine which ones were American and which were Russian. He demonstrated his ability to the United States Navy, which gave him no indication that he had been successful. However, several years later when he tried to get a passport to visit South Africa to dowse for minerals, he was turned down on the grounds that he was a security risk.[3]

Greg Nielsen and Joseph Polansky reported that the United States Marine Corps teach their mine experts how to detect enemy mines by map dowsing.[4]

Map dowsing has been of great help in locating water in desert regions of the world. The Reverend H. W. Lea-Wilson described in an article[5] how he found water for a doctor in a remote part of India. She was very grateful, as it enabled her to expand her practice. After he returned to England, the doctor wrote to him to say that she had moved to a very small village. Could he help her find water there? Mr. Lea-Wilson asked for a plan of the village, which he map dowsed for water. A bore was drilled at the position he suggested and good quality water was found thirty feet below the surface. Mr. Lea-Wilson also located water in Uganda and Sri Lanka from his office in England.[6]

Map dowsers are able to locate anything they set their minds on. George de la Warr was asked to locate methane gas in the Himalayas by the Indian government. He successfully did this by map dowsing from the comfort of his home in Oxford, England.[7]

New Zealand water-diviner Brian Reid had an interesting experience the very first time he tried divining over a map. A woman whom he had not met before placed a large map of Germany in front of him and asked him to tell her where she had been born. He told her that it was impossible to do that, but she insisted. Brian Reid used his brass angle rods on the map and finally pinpointed a spot. With horror, he noticed that it was in the middle of a river. He started to apologize, but the woman said, "You're right. I was born on a river boat."[8]

To perform map dowsing, obtain the largest scale map you can of the area you are planning to dowse. Some people say that your map has to be oriented to face north. In my experience, it makes no difference at all. The map is simply another tool that can be used to make your dowsing easier.

Sit down comfortably at a table with your map in front of you. The table should be of a convenient height so that you can rest your right elbow comfortably on it. Hold your pendulum in your right hand, if you are right-handed. Rest your left elbow on the table and hold the pendulum in your left hand if you are left-handed (See Figure 4A).

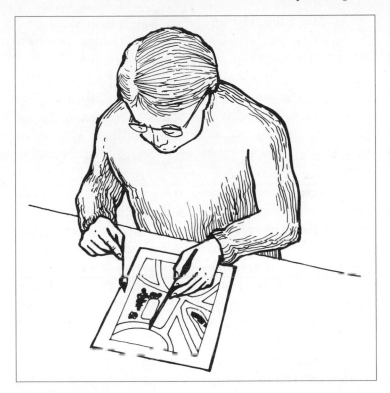

Figure 4A: Map Dowsing

Begin by asking your pendulum if the item you are dowsing for is in the area covered by the map. If you get a positive response, carry onto the next stage.

Think about the item you are searching for and gradually go over the map with an object in your left hand to act as a pointer. Usually, a pen or pencil works well for this. With small scale maps, a pin might be more appropriate.

As you work, try and visualize the area in your mind. I frequently go into an almost trance-like state and vividly "see" the area I am dowsing over.

When your pointer is directly over an area that contains whatever it is you are searching for, your pendulum will give you a positive response. In my case, this is a clockwise circular motion. (Remember to ask your pendulum to give you a "yes" response before you start.)

Abbé Mermet suggests that when you first start experimenting with map dowsing, you place the pointer directly over objects that are marked on the map, and ask your pendulum questions about them. For instance, if you are looking for water, hold the pointer over a river, stream, spring, or well that is indicated on the map, and ask your pendulum if this is a supply of water. It should react positively. However, you need to remain aware that the conditions of the land may have changed since the map was drawn. A well or stream may have dried up. When this happens, you can transcend time itself and ask, "Was water available here at the time this map was drawn?" Then ask, "Is water available here now?" If you get a negative response to something that is shown on the map, try to visit the place to confirm what the pendulum is telling you.

GRID METHOD

There are a number of ways to completely cover the map. If the map is divided into grids, it is a simple matter to ask, "Will I find (whatever it is) in this square?"

Once you get a positive response, you can redraw that complete square, place a grid over it and go through the procedure again. You can repeat this as many times as necessary until you find the exact location of the object you are dowsing for.

COORDINATES METHOD

Ask your pendulum, "Where on the north-south coordinate is (whatever it is) to be found?" At the same time, run your pointer slowly down the map from north to south. Mark where the pendulum gives a positive response.

Repeat the process going from west to east.

Where the two coordinates meet is where the object will be found. I usually do a final check by placing the pointer on the exact spot indicated and asking the pendulum, "Will I find (whatever it is) at this location?"

TRIANGULATION METHOD

You need a ruler as well as a pendulum for this method. Start by placing the pendulum over one of the bottom corners of the map and ask the pendulum to indicate the direction of the object for which you are searching.

Once the pendulum is indicating a specific direction, line your ruler up from the corner in the same direction as the swing line. Draw a pencil line across the map using the edge of the ruler.

Repeat the process from the other bottom corner. Where the two pencil lines cross is where the item

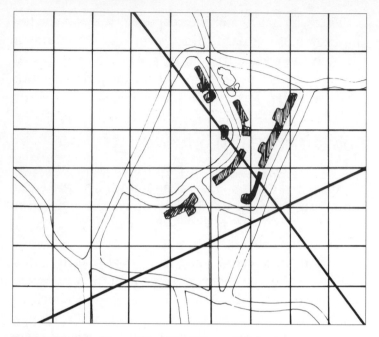

Figure 4B: Map Dowsed by Triangulation Method

will be found (See Figure 4B). Again, you can check this by placing your pointer at this position and asking the pendulum if this is the correct spot.

ADDITIONAL QUESTIONS

Locating the correct site is only part of what can be done with map dowsing. You can continue asking the pendulum questions indefinitely. If you are divining for water, once you have located it, ask the pendulum how deep the water is, how much volume you can get every minute, and what the quality is like.

Once you have located a position on the map, try to visit the actual site to confirm your findings. When I first began map dowsing, I was rather skeptical about it, so I tended to ignore what I had discovered from the map, and went through the normal process on the site. I very quickly learned how accurate map dowsing could be. On my first attempt, I traced the path of a water course on a hilly farm. The map did not really give me an accurate picture of just how rough the terrain was. I found the water course in a matter of minutes, sitting comfortably at home with a map and pendulum. It took five hours of tramping and climbing to reach the correct spot in the field. It is not an easy matter to traverse rough country when your hands are occupied with dowsing equipment!

It is not always necessary to have an accurate map. A sketch or plan will work just as well. Abbé Mermet told how he successfully located a missing cow from a roughly drawn sketch of the area. After locating the exact position of the cow the Abbé continued asking questions of his pendulum and was able to tell the astounded farmer that his cow had fallen into a precipice one hundred meters deep. He said she was lying there with her four legs in the air. The farmer had not been aware of this precipice, but when he visited the spot indicated by Abbé Mermet he found the cow, with all four legs in the air![9]

You can dowse for anything at all using maps. My friend Docc Hilford, in Arizona, uses a map to locate arrowheads and pottery shards in the desert. You can use it to trace missing people or animals. Recently, I helped some friends find their missing kitten by dows-

Figure 4C: Map Dowsing Using a Pendulum

ing over a street map of their locality. An acquaintance of mine map dowses to locate gold, silver and other precious metals. Abbé Mermet was extremely good at locating oil around the world. He also conducted important archaeological dowsing in Rome, from his office in France. The records of his successes are in the Vatican Library Archives. Electricity and telephone cables are easily located by map dowsing.

How Does It Work?

Many people who accept the feasibility of dowsing scoff at the idea of holding a pendulum over a map. They are not giving our incredible minds enough credit. Our subconscious minds are in contact with the universal mind, which knows everything. That is why we can go to bed with a problem that seems unsolvable, and wake up in the morning with the answer. While we are asleep, our subconscious mind works on the problem and gains the answer from the universal mind.

Map dowsing can be seen as a type of clairvoyance. The pendulum acts as an extension to our nervous system and gives us the correct answer. All the same, it is easy to fool ourselves. We need to trust the pendulum implicitly.

A woman I know was trying to track down her ⸿⸿⸿⸿⸿ ⸿⸿⸿⸿⸿⸿⸿ ⸿ ⸿⸿⸿ ⸿⸿⸿⸿ ⸿⸿⸿⸿⸿⸿⸿⸿ ⸿⸿⸿ ⸿⸿⸿ ⸿⸿ ⸿⸿⸿ daughter had run away with a boyfriend whom the mother did not like. She was unhappy about this, but expected her to return home in a day or two. When this did not happen, she became worried and consulted her pendulum.

She began by asking the pendulum if her daughter was safe. The pendulum gave a positive answer to this. She then asked if her daughter was in a nearby town where the boyfriend lived. The pendulum gave a negative answer. The mother continued to ask questions, asking if her daughter was in a variety of nearby towns. One of these gave a positive response. However, the mother ignored this response as she thought it unlikely that the young couple would have traveled there.

She found a map of the town where the young man had his home and began dowsing it. The pendulum gave a positive response at the street where the young man lived.

The woman immediately phoned the boy's parents and demanded to speak to her daughter.

"She's not here," she was told.

The mother got in her car and drove to the town to check for herself. The boy's parents had not seen or heard from the couple and were just as worried as she was.

The mother returned home, arriving there at the same time as her daughter and boyfriend. They had been staying with friends in the small town that the mother's pendulum had indicated, but which she had discarded as a possibility.

If the mother had accepted what the pendulum had told her, and then consulted a map of that town, she would have been able to locate her daughter. As it was, she let her logical mind dismiss what the pendulum was telling her.

When the mother dowsed over the town where the young man lived, the pendulum reacted over his street because it was what she wanted it to do. She was using her mind to influence the pendulum, an example of psychokinesis.

Try to ensure when you are doing any sort of dowsing that you do not allow your mind to influence the instrument.

Here is an experiment that demonstrates how easy it is to influence your dowsing equipment, and consequently fool yourself.

Spread a map in front of you and place a short piece of cotton on it, well away from any source of water. Tell yourself that this piece of cotton is an underground stream of water.

Move your pointer across the map and when it moves over the piece of cotton, your pendulum will start to give a positive response. This is purely because you had told your mind that it was an underground stream.

Now, remove the cotton, but tell yourself that the underground stream is still there. You will find that your pendulum still gives a positive response when your pointer passes over the spot.

Finally, tell yourself that the piece of cotton was simply a piece of cotton thread, and not an underground stream. Dowse again and your pendulum will not react.

Isn't it amazing how our minds can cause this to happen? Even experienced dowsers fool themselves at times when they expect to find something at a certain place.

I remember about twenty years ago when I was vacationing in the high country of the South Island of New Zealand. I met a farmer who was complaining of how dry the weather was, and how badly he needed water. I offered to dowse for him, and he explained that other dowsers had already tried without success. However, if I would like to try, he would be very grateful. After a pleasant hour or two walking around his large property I paused for a rest. To my right was a large bluff, and it looked to me as if it had been caused by a large river that must have run around it long ago. The rest of the landscape seemed to bear out this hypothesis, so I moved closer to the bluff and sure enough, my angle rods crossed over each other.

I was very pleased with myself, as I thought I had been saved from hours of exploration on the farm. However, my delight was short-lived when I tried to find the direction of this water source. My angle rods did not move at all when I walked in a large circle around the spot.

When I returned to the spot I had marked, I asked my angle rods, "Am I fooling myself?" The rods promptly crossed each other.

When I returned to the farmhouse, the farmer told me that several other dowsers had had positive reactions near the bluff, but that the river had moved several miles since the bluff had been formed. I, and the other dowsers, had assumed water would be found at that spot because the terrain showed that a river had been there in the past. We let our eyes and minds influence our dowsing rods. It was a valuable lesson for me.

CHAPTER FIVE

The Amazing Pendulum

It is a common misconception that most dowsers use a forked stick as a divining rod. In fact, much more dowsing is done with a pendulum than with a rod.

The pendulum has been known for thousands of years. Marcellinus, who was the pope from about A.D. 296 until his death in 304,[1] wrote that a ring suspended on a thread in the middle of a tripod decorated with snakes and other animals was being used in the first century A.D. Roman letters were arranged around the circumference of the tripod and the ring was reputed to swing from one letter to another and spell out the answers to questions. This appears to be a combination of the pendulum and ouija board.

In his history of the Roman Empire, Marcellinus included an account of a priest using a ring swinging on a thread to determine who was going to succeed Emperor Valens. The ring was suspended over a circular platter which contained the letters of the alphabet around the rim. The impromptu pendulum moved first to T, then H, E and O, telling the conspirators that the next emperor would be Theodorus. Emperor

Figure 5A: Example of a Pendulum Suspended from a Chain

Valens heard about the plot and several of the conspirators whose names happened to begin with "Theo" were put to death. Somehow, a man called Theodosius was overlooked. He eventually became emperor, making the prophesy of the pendulum come true.

The use of the pendulum as a divination device continued, and in 1326 Pope John XXII issued a bull decrying its use, claiming that it "obtained answers in the manner of the Devil."[2]

The Science Museum in South Kensington, London, contains a collection of emblematic tools that were used by the various guilds in Saxony in the seventeenth and early eighteenth centuries. One engraving depicts two men with dowsing rods facing another man with a large pendulum. This is believed to be the first documented evidence of the pendulum as a dowsing device.[3]

In the early nineteenth century, interest in the pendulum grew in scientific circles.

Johann Wilhelm Ritter, today mainly remembered as the father of electrochemistry, studied the pendulum in Italy. Interestingly, he failed to get a response from the pendulum until Francesco Campetti, his teacher, laid a hand on his shoulder.

Ritter found that the pendulum acted in a different fashion over the north pole of a magnet than it did over the south. He later concluded that everything contained a special signature, as the pendulum almost always acted in a specific fashion when held over different objects. A lemon, for instance, caused the pendulum to create a specific, distinctive pattern. This same pattern would be repeated over other lemons, but the pattern would be different with an orange, a piece of zinc, or anything else. Also, the movements would be different when the pendulum was held over different parts of the same object.

This research naturally led him to study the polarities of the human body, so he could arguably claim to be the first radiesthetist. Like most innovators, he was ridiculed by others in the academic establishment. However, he persevered and became the first person to demonstrate that the pendulum can tap the universal mind and provide answers to any question. Naturally, these questions had to be formulated so they could be answered with a positive or negative response. Ritter emphasized that the questioner had to be sincere and ask only serious questions.

Ritter's perseverance in the face of ridicule encouraged Professor Antoine Gerboin of the University of Strasbourg to publish a book that contained 253 tests that could be done with a pendulum. Professor Gerboin became interested in the subject after he was given a pendulum on a visit to India.

This book, in turn, intrigued Michel-Eugene Chevreul, who spent twenty years studying the subject. In fact, even today the pendulum is often referred to as "Chevreul's pendulum."

Chevreul decided to test if the movement of the pendulum was caused by involuntary muscular responses of the arm. He did this by supporting his arm on a block of wood at various places from his shoulder to the hand. The movement of the pendulum decreased the closer the block of wood came to the hand, and in fact, stopped completely when the fingers that held the pendulum were also resting on the piece of wood.

This could have ended the matter for Chevreul, but one thing bothered him. He found that by gazing at the pendulum as he used it, he would enter a different state of awareness. He concluded that there was a definite relationship between the thoughts of the dowser and the movements of the pendulum. Chevreul could have taken this a step further, but his conservative, scientific background would not allow it, and his ultimate findings were negative.

It was left to others to prove that the pendulum could be moved by the power of thought alone.

Experiments with the Pendulum

There are thousands of tests that can be done with the pendulum.[4] A few are included here to give you some idea of the amazing things that you can do with your pendulum. Most of these tests require someone else to assist you, and it is a good idea to take turns with the pendulum. That way, you will both remain interested and be able to measure your progress with someone else.

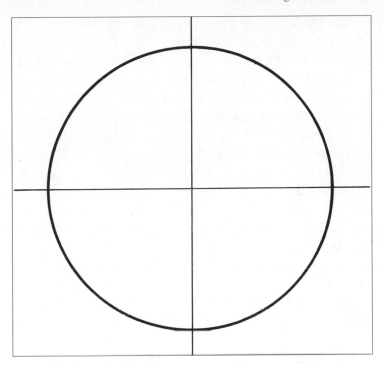

Figure 5B: Circle in Four Parts for Dowsing

MENTAL INFLUENCE

For this test, use either Figure 5B or, alternatively, draw a circle with a large plus sign in the middle of it.

Hold the pendulum about an inch over the center of the plus sign. Relax and then ask it to move to and fro in a north-south movement. After a few moments, your pendulum will start to move in the direction you are thinking about.

While it is still moving in this direction, start thinking that you want the pendulum to change direction and move in an east-west direction. You will notice the pendulum gradually change direction until the pendulum is moving strongly from side to side.

After watching this for a short while, start thinking about the pendulum moving in a clockwise circular motion. The pendulum will quickly do this. Finally, ask it to move around the circle in an anti-clockwise direction.

As you perform this experiment, ensure that you are not consciously making the pendulum move. We want the pendulum to be moved solely by the influence of your mind.

You will find that the pendulum will react to your thoughts more quickly each time you do this experiment. The movements will also increase.

ATTRACT AND REPEL

You will need three coins for this experiment, two of the same denomination and preferably of the same date, and one as different from the others as possible. You might choose to use two quarters and a penny, for instance.

Place the two coins of the same denomination on the table in front of you, three or four inches apart. Hold the pendulum between the two coins. You will find that the pendulum will start to move and oscillate between the two coins. Once you have a marked to-and-fro movement, ask a friend to replace one of the two coins with the other coin while the pendulum is still oscillating.

You will immediately notice that the movement of the pendulum changes sharply, as if the new coin were repelling the pendulum. Once you have noted the change in the pendulum, have your friend replace the original coin and you will find the pendulum will return to its original oscillation.

This was a favorite test of Tom Lethbridge, distinguished archaeologist, author and dowser.[5]

Try this test again with your eyes closed. Open them to verify that your pendulum is oscillating between the two identical coins. Then close your eyes and have a friend change one of the coins as silently as possible. When you open your eyes again, you will find that your pendulum is rejecting the influence of the new coin.

WHERE IS THE COIN?

This test requires three or four cups and a coin. Ask a friend to turn the cups upside down and place the coin under any one of them while you are not looking.

Hold the pendulum over each cup and silently ask it to tell you if the coin is underneath. The pendulum will give a positive response to the correct cup and a negative response to the others. You can repeat this by adding more and more cups.

If you find this test hard to do, try it again, holding a coin of the same denomination to the one under the cup in your free hand. You will find that the coin in your hand will help you find the other one. This extra coin is called a "witness."

Interestingly enough, John Mullins, the celebrated English dowser, was able to do this experiment using a forked twig, rather than a pendulum. He claimed to be able to locate nothing but water with his dowsing rod. However, Mr. T. Forder Plowman wrote that he had seen Mullins successfully find three gold sovereigns hidden under the carpet with his dowsing rod. John Mullins insisted that he was receiving a response to water, but the coins were found directly under the three positions where his rod reacted.[6]

A more advanced version of this experiment convinced a renowned skeptic of the reality of dowsing. Abbé Alberto Fortis was an Augustinian abbot who left the monastery and became secretary of the National Institute of Italy. As a sophisticated, well-read scientist, he regarded dowsing as only a source of great amusement, until he attended a dinner party in Naples. Pierre Thouvenel, a renowned physician and researcher, was also present. Thouvenel was convinced of the reality of dowsing and agreed to allow his best subject to be tested by the abbot. Fortis asked a friend to take a small sack of silver coins and secretly bury them somewhere in the grounds of Fortis' house. Pennet, the dowser, located the sack of coins with no difficulty at all. Abbé Fortis, who was later shown many more demonstrations by this talented dowser, recalled: "I reddened when I recalled that I previously mocked something about which I knew nothing."[7]

LOCATE THE OBJECT

Ask a friend to choose several objects and arrange them in a row on a table. While your back is turned, your friend is to pick up one of the items and hold it in his or her hands for fifteen or twenty seconds, and then replace it.

Dowse each of the items in turn, silently asking your pendulum if this is the object your friend held. You will find that your pendulum will almost invariably tell you the correct object.

Once you get good at this, ask your friend to simply think of one of the objects. You will find that your pendulum will be just as successful at locating the correct object.

LOCATE THE OBJECT, MARK TWO

For this test, simply ask your friend to choose any object in the room. There is no need to hold your pendulum over any of the items. Suspend the pendulum and ask it questions. "Is it the lamp?" "Is it the carpet?" "Is it the window?" The game is a little like the children's game of "I spy," except that it is the pendulum that tells you "yes" or "no."

With this test you can either try to locate the object by simply picking items at random, or you can gradually pin it down. You may, for instance, start by asking if the object is in this half of the room. Then you may ask, "Is it near the bookcase?" "Is it near the door?" When you get a positive answer to this, you can gradually move closer and closer. If you got a positive response to the bookcase, you might ask, "Is it on the bookcase?" If that is also positive, you can ask about each shelf in turn, until you finally name the correct item.

LOCATE THE OBJECT, MARK THREE

This time, ask your friend to choose anything that is in the house. Determine the correct room with your pendulum, and then proceed as in version two, until you name the item chosen.

HOW MANY?

Ask your friend to place any number of coins under a cup. There are two ways for your pendulum to tell you the number of coins. You can ask your pendulum, "Are there more than five coins?" You can now proceed by inquiring about different numbers one at a time.

Alternatively, you can suspend your pendulum inside a tumbler and ask the pendulum to tell you the correct number of coins. The pendulum will move from side to side, tapping against the glass the same number of times as there are coins.

PACK OF CARDS TEST

Start by removing the Jokers and then ask your friend to select any card from a deck of cards. Now ask your pendulum, "Is it a red card?" If the answer is positive, you know the card must be a heart or a diamond. "Is it a diamond?" A negative answer tells you the card is a heart. "Is it a court card?" (Jack, Queen or King.) If the answer is negative, you can go through the numbers one at a time until the pendulum gives you a positive response.

We remove the Jokers first to eliminate any mistakes that could occur if you forget about this particular card. If you start by asking if the card is a red one, and the pendulum says "no," you are likely to assume that it must therefore be a black card. However, if you have not removed the Jokers, this may not be the case.

You can do this experiment just as well without a pack of cards. Simply ask your friend to think of a playing card and your pendulum will be able to tell you which card it is.

THE KINGS AND QUEENS

Take out all the kings and queens from a deck of playing cards and shuffle them. Place them in a row face-down. Suspend your pendulum over each card, one at a time, and see if you can separate the kings from the queens. Some people prefer to place each card in an envelope, and then mix the envelopes, just in case they subconsciously pick up imperfections on the backs of the playing cards.

The same test can also be done with photographs of men and women. Again, mix the photographs up and see if you can separate the sexes.

THE INVISIBLE WALL

Ask two friends to visualize an imaginary wall inside a room, while you are elsewhere. They are to think about the wall once you return, but give you no conscious clues. You will find that your pendulum will locate the wall, even though it is just an imaginary one constructed in the minds of your friends. This test certainly demonstrates that thoughts are things.

WHICH IS WHICH?

This final test provides good practice for map dowsing. Again, you need three cups and three different objects that will fit under them. Ask your friend to place a different object under each cup. Now, using your pendulum, you can find out which object is under which cup.

Suppose the three objects are a coin, a pea, and a hazelnut. Suspend your pendulum over the first cup and ask, "Is the coin under this cup?" No matter what response the pendulum gives you, continue with, "Is the pea under this cup?" Finally, ask about the hazel nut. Your pendulum will have given you a positive response for one of the items.

Do the same thing with the second cup. By the time you come to the third cup you should know what is under it, as it will be the one item that has drawn a negative response over the other two cups. However, you may wish to confirm your previous choices by asking the questions again over the third cup.

These simple tests all provide good practice with the pendulum. They are designed to not only give you confidence in handling the pendulum, but also to allow you to see just how accurate the pendulum's answers are.

You will be able to create many more tests of your own. These experiments are really just "party tricks." The pendulum is much too important an instrument to use as a plaything. Regard these tests as opportunities to practice and to develop your skills, rather than as an opportunity to perform or show off to others.

THE AUTHOR DEMONSTRATES USING THE PENDULUM.

You will find plenty of opportunities to practice in daily life as well. Next time you lose your car keys ask your pendulum to tell you where they are. If you have a choice of a number of locations for your summer vacation, ask the pendulum which place you would enjoy most. If you are interested in taking a cooking course, but find it hard to choose between Chinese or Mexican, ask your pendulum. Follow the advice your pendulum gives you. It will not lead you astray.

CHAPTER SIX

Hand and Body Dowsing

It is likely that body dowsing was the earliest known method of dowsing. Cave men had to find water to survive and, being more in touch with their bodies than we are today, they probably simply allowed their bodies to lead them towards sources of water.

Many animals are able to do this, also. Elephants are sometimes followed in times of drought as they head unerringly towards a supply of underground water which they dig down to with their tusks.[1] The donkey is said to possess a similar talent. He points his head towards water, heads to the underground source beneath the sand and digs down to it with his hooves.[2]

The ability that salmon have to return to their birthplace to spawn could well be an example of dowsing. Perhaps swallows dowse their way back to Capistrano. The migration of birds is still largely a mystery. The sun is certainly used as a compass, but other factors also seem to play a part. Scientists hypothesize that magnetism or electricity may also be involved. Even more remarkable than bird migration is how monarch butterflies are able to fly from South America to the exact same tree in Santa Cruz, California, three generations after leaving.

Ant hills are almost always built over underground streams. Cats enjoy sleeping over water, but most other animals try to avoid it.

Consequently, the ability to locate water appears to be common in the animal kingdom. Some humans also seem to have this faculty naturally, though most need a dowsing instrument of some kind to act as an indicator.

Many hand and body dowsers receive a clear picture in their minds of what is below the surface. In 1963, Pieter Van Jaarsveld, a twelve-year-old South African, became internationally famous for his skill at locating water and diamonds. This hand dowser became known as "the boy with X-ray eyes," as he could apparently "see" water "shimmering like green moonlight" under the ground. He found it hard to understand that other people could not see what he could.[3]

Although only a few people seem to have this ability naturally, everyone has the potential to develop it with practice. It is a skill well worth developing. You may be out somewhere without your dowsing equipment. If you can hand or body dowse, you can dowse anywhere you happen to be. Sometimes, you may wish to dowse without drawing attention to yourself. For instance, you may be at a popular tourist site, such as an ancient cathedral or monument. Years ago, I did some dowsing at Fountains Abbey in Yorkshire. It was a beautiful summer's day and hundreds of people were there. I was able to quietly hand dowse with few people even being aware of it.

HAND DOWSING

The best way to practice using your hands is to dowse for objects that you have already located by other means. If, for instance, you have successfully dowsed for your water mains using a pendulum or rod, go over the same ground again with your hands and arms extended in front of you at shoulder height, with your palms facing each other. Some people prefer to have the arms fully extended, others prefer to hold the upper arms against the body with only the forearms and hands extended.

Move slowly towards the place where you know the water pipe is. Keep as relaxed as you can. If you are fortunate, you may experience some tingling, itching or involuntary movement in your hands as you get close to the pipe. You may find that one arm starts to rise of its own accord. It may even bob up and down as if it has developed a life of its own.

Obviously, walking for any length of time with both arms extended can be very tiring. Consequently, many hand dowsers extend just one arm. When it gets tired, they extend the other one.

Do not be concerned if you experience no sensation at all. Try again, but this time wiggle your hands slightly and see if this makes a difference. Another variation is to extend one arm with the shoulder, arm and hand muscles held as tightly as possible. When you are over the target object, this arm will start to

THE AUTHOR HAND DOWSING.

vibrate and move uncontrollably. No wonder hand-dowsers are sometimes called hand tremblers!

Another method is to hold your hands out in front of you, a body width apart, with the palms facing each other. As you approach the object you are dowsing for, the hands will slowly move together until they almost touch.[4]

Experiment by making your hands into impromptu V-shaped rods. You do this by making fists of your hands and extending your thumbs. Push your thumbs together at a ninety degree angle and hold your hands with the thumbs pointing towards your body. Keep reasonable pressure on both thumbs. When you are over the item you are dowsing for, your thumbs will suddenly point downwards. Some people notice their hands start to vibrate slightly as they get close to the object they are divining.

Another way is to turn your arms into a large V-shape by clasping your hands together and extending your arms. The arms will start to vibrate when you are over the object you are dowsing for. This is the method that Fred Rodwell, the boy who achieved fame as a dowser in England in the 1880s, usually used. His hands would lock together so tightly that he could not separate them until he moved away from the site where the dowsing response occurred.

Cynthia Plowdon, a dowser in Somerset, England, extends her forefingers and presses them together to create a small V-shape. Her arms are bent at the elbows and her hands are held at chest height. In her case, the dowsing response is a sudden tightening of all the muscles in her arms and she cannot separate her forefingers until she has moved away from the item she is dowsing for. Some people who use their forefingers in this way hold their hands at forehead height. Dowsing responses vary from person to person. I have watched an elderly man dowse with his forefingers in exactly the same way as Cynthia Plowdon. However, in his case, the dowsing response was a rapid up-and-down movement of his forefingers.

Leicester Gataker, a well-known early twentieth-century English dowser, used to walk briskly over the area he was dowsing with his arms hanging down and slightly outwards. His dowsing response was a vibration in the middle fingers of each hand.[5]

Raymond Willey, in his book *Modern Dowsing*, describes a method used in India. The hands are held palms upwards with the insides of the wrists touching the sides of the body at waist level. The fingers are extended and the arms are held rigid. When the dowser is over the item he or she is searching for, the hands move up and down spasmodically.[5]

I have not seen this method myself, but several years ago I saw an Indian dowser doing something similar. He held his arms out in front of him, bent at the elbow, and rested his right wrist on the left one. He pushed down with his right wrist and upwards with the left, creating tension in his arms. When he was over the object he was dowsing for, his fingers and hands would vibrate uncontrollably. He called this "butterfly dowsing" as the movements of his hands and fingers looked exactly like a panic-stricken butterfly.

A final form of hand-dowsing is one used by a Yorkshire dowser who dowsed with a coin resting in the palm of his hand. When standing over the object he was dowsing for, the coin would turn over in his hand.[6]

You may find hand dowsing comes naturally to you. Most people find it difficult at first, but it becomes easier with practice. Abbé Bouly, a leading French dowser in the first half of this century, said in a speech he gave in 1928: "I no longer require a rod, I can see the stream with my eyes; I attune my mind."[7]

BODY DOWSING

With body dowsing the entire body provides a dowsing response. This may come in different ways. Profuse perspiration, tightening of muscles, hairs rising on

THE AUTHOR SEARCHES FOR A DIRECTION BY HAND DOWSING.

arms and legs, giddiness and tingling sensations are some of the different sensations that body dowsers experience. Naturally, each dowser does not experiences all of the above indications. A friend of mine experiences the hairs of his arms rising and a feeling that he is going to faint as a dowsing response. He has never fainted while dowsing, but has come close to it on several occasions.

To become an effective body dowser, you need to be extremely aware of your physical body. Think about the object you are dowsing for and then remain alert for any changes that occur in your body. This is most likely to be a sudden tightening of a muscle, but as we are all unique, your response could be something completely different.

A friend of mine uses a mixture of hand and body dowsing when he searches for water. He starts by standing on the edge of the area he is planning to dowse. He extends one arm and slowly moves it in a semi-circle. His arm starts trembling when he is pointing at a source of water. He then walks in the direction his arm indicated until the muscles of his back suddenly tighten. This tells him that he is standing directly over a source of underground water. In his case, the muscle tightening is quite extreme and I have seen the muscles of his back become so tight that it took his wife thirty minutes of massage to loosen them.

My friend's experience is similar to that of Hans Wolff, a dowser from Freiberg, who was tested back in 1713. He dowsed for veins of metal by making a fist of his right hand and extending his right arm. When he came near a vein, his arm would shake violently. When he was standing directly over the vein, his entire body would shake and tremble. His examiners could not understand how he was able to work in mines where veins of metals constantly surrounded him. Hans Wolff's answer was hundreds of years ahead of his times. He told the examiners that if he did not focus his thoughts on finding a vein of ore, he experienced no reaction when crossing over or working near one.[8]

I use body dowsing in quite a different way. If I am in a store and am not sure whether or not to purchase a certain item, I close my eyes and ask myself if I should buy it. If I should, I find myself leaning towards the item. If I should not buy it I tend to lean away. This is an example of dowsing being made very practical in day to day life. We could, actually, be doing this unconsciously all the time. If you went to a party and met someone who was very interesting and attractive you would tend to lean towards this person while conversing. If you met someone who was unappealing, you would tend to lean backwards, away from the person.

I also body dowse when I have to make a choice between two or more items. If I am in a bookstore and am interested in two books, but have only enough money on me to buy one, I close my eyes and ask myself which one I should buy today. My body will lean towards one of the books, telling me which one to purchase. This is certainly more discreet than holding a pendulum over the books in the store.

Good body dowsers are very sensitive and are aware of their bodies all the time. An acquaintance of mine lost an emerald brooch that she had inherited from her mother. The brooch was not an expensive one, but had enormous personal value and my friend was upset when it disappeared. Two months later, she was having morning tea at her sister's house and her right forefinger started to vibrate slightly.

"It's here! It's here!" she called out with great excitement. Sure enough, the lost brooch was found under a cushion on the chair she was sitting on. On her previous visit, two months earlier, she had sat on the same chair and the brooch must have fallen off and ended up under a cushion. It would probably still be there if she had not immediately recognized the slight movement of her finger as being a dowsing response.

Unless hand and body dowsing is something you find completely natural and easy to do, you will need to practice and persevere. It is an extremely useful skill and will well repay any amount of work you put into perfecting it.

CHAPTER SEVEN

How Does It Work?

For some two hundred years, people have known that involuntary movements of the hands cause the dowsing rods and pendulums to move. Chevreul proved that with his experiments.

However, we do not know what causes the hands to move in this fashion. In some cases, the movements have been so strong, even violent, that dowsers have been injured.

We know that our thoughts can influence the pendulum. We can make the pendulum move from side to side by willing it to do so. Our mind is creating the involuntary movements necessary to cause the pendulum to move in the direction we want it to.

Because our mind is able to do this, it is perhaps not so surprising that it can also answer questions by tapping into the universal mind.

Our logical, conscious mind lives in the real world and deals with facts and things that can be proven. Our inner, subconscious mind is much larger and contains memories of everything that has ever happened to us. It also looks after such important matters as ensuring we breathe and that our hearts keep on beating. Fortunately, we do not have to remain consciously aware of this. Our subconscious mind looks after all of this for us.

Our subconscious mind also has access to the universal mind, which has knowledge of everything. This is why we can go to bed at night with a problem that seems impossible to solve, and wake up in the morning with the answer. During our sleep, our subconscious mind has asked for the answer from the universal mind, and has it all ready for us when we awaken the next morning.

This is an oversimplification, of course. Yet it shows that we do have access to any information that we require, anything at all.

When we are dowsing for water or oil, we do not know exactly where we will find it. But the universal mind knows, as it knows everything. Consequently, if we dowse in a mood of confident anticipation that our rods will let us know when we find the item we are searching for, our subconscious mind will get the answer from the universal mind and let us know by an involuntary movement that makes the dowsing rod move.

Docc Hilford, a dowser in Arizona, uses angle rods to locate arrowheads and pottery shards in the desert. He believes that we see much more than we register in our minds. We look, but do not always see. Consequently, when his angle rods lead him directly to an ancient pottery shard, he believes that he probably saw the shard with his eyes, but did not consciously register the fact. This phenomena is called hyperacucia, which describes the ability to be aware of minute details that most people would not see. Not all of the information being taken into the brain is passed on to the conscious awareness.

We all register visual clues in the same way. For instance, if we are searching for water, we may subconsciously notice that the vegetation is lusher or different in a certain part of the area we are dowsing. Once I was dowsing for water while my wife was talking with a passerby. During the conversation she told this man where she thought the water would be found. I was not aware of this, but my dowsing rod indicated exactly the same spot. She had deduced the position by simply looking at the vegetation. I was so immersed in my dowsing rod that I was scarcely aware of my surroundings.

Consequently, use of visual clues is a solution that is sometimes put forward to explain dowsing. Certainly, this could be the case some of the time. After all, it is common for substances underground to effect changes on the surface.

But it does not explain how a dowser can find, for instance, underground power lines or detect oil by map dowsing.

Dowsers, themselves, find it hard to agree on what makes it work. Many feel that it is an electromagnetic attraction between the dowsing rod and the item they are searching for. Certainly, the downward (or sometimes upward) pull is strong enough to make many dowsers feel that some sort of magnetic attraction is at work. Albert Einstein thought that dowsing was probably the result of an electromagnetic attraction.[1] Dr. John Zimmerman, of the University of Colorado Health Sciences Center in Denver, demonstrated that the brain's magnetic fields are strongest when the person is in a relaxed, meditative state or asleep. Solco Tromp, a Dutch geologist, used magnetometers to show that dowsers are unusually sensitive to the earth's magnetic field.[2]

We all possess minute traces of iron in the ethnoid bone, located between our eyes. Dolphins and pigeons also have iron in their ethnoid bones. Scientific experiments show that these minuscule traces of iron act as a directional indicator. The tests used volunteers who were blindfolded and spun around until they were giddy. They were then asked to try and face north. Some failed, but most of the volunteers were able to do this. However, none of them succeeded when a magnet was held close to their heads. A small square of aluminum foil attached to the center of the forehead also has the same effect. It is possible that these tiny traces of iron play a part in dowsing.

However, magnetic attraction does not explain how a competent dowser can provide a variety of additional information, such as the depth, volume and direction of water flow.

Dr. Zaboj V. Harvalik, a Czechoslovakian physicist who taught at the University of Missouri, performed some fascinating experiments in the 1960s. He discovered that his dowsing rod always reacted to electric wires on the ground. He wondered if his rod could also pick up electrical impulses below the surface. He experimented by driving two lengths of waterpipe vertically into the ground sixty feet apart. He attached the exposed ends to a large battery. His dowsing rod responded immediately when he turned on the battery. He tested his friends and found that they all were successful as long as the current was above 20 milliamps. One fifth of his friends could detect a current as low as 2 milliamps, and some could even detect a half milliamp. He found that almost everyone improved with practice, and that everyone dowsed better if they drank a few glasses of water beforehand. He also discovered that people with apparently no dowsing ability could dowse successfully after drinking half a glass of whiskey! The alcohol relaxed them enough to suspend disbelief and become effective dowsers. Dr. Harvalik concluded that the body was essentially a magnetic detector.[3]

One of Dr. Harvalik's most interesting discoveries came when he tested a German dowser, Wilhelm de Boer. De Boer could detect one thousandth of a milliamp. He could even tune into any radio station that Harvalik cared to name. De Boer would slowly turn around in a circle until he was facing the direction of the radio station. Dr. Harvalik would then confirm the accuracy of this by turning his radio in the direction de Boer was facing. This proof that a dowser could select whatever it was he or she wanted to pick up was of vital importance. Skeptics had always scoffed at dowsers' claims that they could pick up anything they chose to concentrate on. De Boer was able to ignore all the other radio frequencies and pick up the very ones Harvalik named.[4]

Dr. Harvalik then began experimenting with dowsing for brainwave rhythms. He constructed a screen in his garden which he stood in front of with earplugs in his ears. People would walk towards him from the other side of the screen and Harvalik's rod would indicate their presence when they were still ten feet away. Interestingly, when his volunteers thought exciting thoughts—such as sex, for instance—Harvalik's rod would detect them from twenty feet away. We have all had the experience of becoming aware that someone is staring at us and turning our heads to see who it is. Dr. Harvalik's experiment demonstrates that this is an example of body dowsing.[5]

Dr. Harvalik hypothesized that electro-magnetism was what made dowsing work. However, he also discovered that he could map-dowse successfully, and electro-magnetism cannot explain his results with a map and pendulum.

Many dowsers believe that everything vibrates in an individual manner, and it is these vibrations that are being picked up subconsciously by the dowser and revealed by the dowsing instrument. Louis Turenne was the first to propound this theory, and it is one that has been accepted by many, including Abbé Mermet.

There is a further possibility that dowsers are using some sort of psychic power. Many dowsers vehemently deny this possibility. In fact, at one meeting of a dowsing society I belong to, an elderly lady told me that I had no business being there, as I was a psychic! Clairvoyance means knowing what is not known, and dowsing is a good example of this. Professor J. B. Rhine, the famous psychic researcher, felt that dowsing owed more to ESP than to physics.

A further argument to the psychic hypothesis is that people do better at dowsing when they suspend disbelief. If they are willing to be open-minded, but not credulous, and allow the dowsing rod to do the work, they achieve good results.

The necessity to suspend disbelief is probably why dowsers seldom do well in organized tests. Dowsers seem to pick up and respond to the negative energies from skeptics and fail to achieve their usual results.

Many questions still need to be answered. Fortunately, though, we have come a long way from one early explanation: mischievous devils!

There are many theories as to why dowsing works. Obviously, information is coming into the body of the dowser in some way that science has yet to explain. Unfortunately, scientists in the West remain skeptical because of the lack of proof.

Despite this, dowsers are employed by the Canadian Ministry of Agriculture, UNESCO, and virtually every major pipeline company in America. In Russia, dowsers have been used to find gold in the Northern Caucasus. They did this with aerial dowsing and Soviet scientists reported that 30 percent less drilling was required than with other methods.[6] The military have made good use of dowsers. In the First World War, dowsers found water for the troops in the desert. The Germans used dowsers to follow the movements of British warships in the Second World War.[7] The use of dowsing during the Vietnam War has already been mentioned.

The argument about how dowsing works continues. In the meantime, countless dowsers around the world are successfully finding water, oil, gold, pipes, ancient artifacts, lost property, and countless other items. They are not interested in how it works. They know that it does, and that is enough for them.

Charles Richet, the French physiologist and Nobel Prize winner, summed it up best when he said: "Dowsing is a fact we must accept."[8]

CHAPTER EIGHT

Dowsing for Self-Improvement

Your dowsing skills can be very useful in self-improvement. You can easily dowse your subconscious mind to find which areas of your life need more attention.

Here is an interesting experiment that often provides surprising answers. Sit down in a comfortable place where you will not be interrupted. Rest your elbow on a table and suspend your pendulum. Close you eyes and ask yourself, "Am I happy?" Do not try to analyze the question. Simply ask it and repeat it over and over in your mind for about thirty seconds. Open your eyes and see the answer that the pendulum is indicating.

This particular question is a difficult one. You might have a wonderfully successful relationship, a devoted family and plenty of hobbies and interests. But you hate your job. Would the pendulum say that you were happy in this case? It may, because all of the wonderful, positive aspects of your life might well overrule the one area where you were not happy. Alternatively, if your job irritated you so much that it threatened the other parts of your life, the pendulum might well give a resounding "no."

This first question is all-encompassing. It is useful in that it can give clues that everything is not going as well as you may have thought.

Suppose that you are happy in your work. You have been reasonably successful and have been promoted to a position that you enjoy. You would like to earn a little bit more money, but all the same you are managing to live pretty well on your current income. It might be interesting to ask your pendulum, "Am I progressing as fast as I should be in my chosen career?"

If the pendulum gives a negative answer you can proceed to ask questions that gradually pinpoint the areas where you should be putting in more effort.

You may find that your pendulum tells you that you are working too hard and should spend more time with your loved ones. It might be hard to achieve this if you are bogged down with work, but your pendulum would not tell you this if there wasn't a good reason. Very few people lie on their death-beds saying, "I wish I'd spent more time at work." Work is an important part of most people's lives, but it should not take over to the extent that it threatens relationships and health.

Some months ago, a middle-aged man came to see me. He is a highly successful dentist. During the course of conversation he told me that he had never wanted to be a dentist, but became one as his father had been one and his parents wanted him to follow in the family tradition. Like so many others, he was fulfilling his parents' expectations. He had wanted to be a teacher, but his parents did not regard that as being a sufficiently prestigious or lucrative type of career. So he became a dentist and loathed everything about it.

I gave him a pendulum to hold and we asked it a variety of questions. The pendulum showed that he was on the verge of serious health problems and that he should take time out to think about what he should do with his life. This man is still working as a dentist, but has a plan of where he wants to be two years from now. He intends to be making his living from his hobby of photography. He plans to do this both as a freelance photographer and as a teacher of photography. He has discussed it with his wife and family, and even his parents agree that it is a good thing for him. Already he looks years younger and is full of enthusiasm and zest for life.

Do you look forward to going to work on Monday? Do you look at your watch every five minutes? Do you breathe a sigh of relief when it is Friday? If so, it is time to ask your pendulum some serious questions about your work.

A short while ago a young man came to me complaining that he could make no friends. He was well-groomed, articulate, and reasonably outgoing, and it was hard to believe that he had any difficulties in making friends.

I introduced him to the pendulum and let him ask it different questions. He began by asking, "Would I make a good friend?" The pendulum replied in the negative. After several other negative answers to his questions he asked, "Would I make friends if I gave more of myself?" The pendulum said "yes." "Do I keep too much of myself hidden?" was the next question. Again the answer was "yes." It turned out that this young man had been sexually abused while at camp several years earlier, and ever since then had been wary of making friends with anyone. It took many questions to learn that this was the reason for his problem, but once the pendulum pointed it out, he brightened immediately. "I think I knew that all along, but had somehow hidden it," he told me. "I just know I'll make friends now."

Another instance concerns a young woman. She had been shy all of her life and had recently developed a twitch in her right eye whenever she felt uncomfortable. Unfortunately for her, the twitch made it appear that she was winking, and this frequently put her into potentially embarrassing situations. By using the pendulum, we were able to determine that she felt herself unworthy of love, as she had been discarded by a boyfriend when she was sixteen. Still using the pendulum, we had her inner mind agree that she was a good, worthwhile person. It agreed to help her gain confidence and self-esteem. Over the next few months her confidence increased and her twitch lessened. She is now in a serious relationship and experiences the twitch only when she is overtired.

We can divide our lives into as many categories as we wish. One of the simplest methods is to divide a circle into four quarters. In each quarter write one of these words: physical, mental, social and spiritual.

Place a finger inside one of the quarters and suspend your pendulum to one side of the circle. Close your eyes, relax for a few seconds and then ask, "Am I doing as well as I should be in this area of my life?" Wait for several seconds and then open your eyes and see what the pendulum is saying. Repeat this with the remaining quadrants.

Some people prefer to do this experiment with the pendulum suspended inside each quadrant. Try both methods and see which one works better for you.

You may find that your pendulum tells you that you are not doing as much physically as you should be. If this is the case, ask more questions until you find out what you should be doing. Your pendulum might suggest regular games of squash, or maybe just gentle walks. However, it is then up to you to actually do it. If you have no desire or intention of improving yourself in the areas the pendulum indicates, there is no point in doing the experiments at all.

You may prefer to divide your circle into six sections. These could be labeled: Career, Finances, Physical, Mental, Family, and Spiritual. This is the grouping that I normally use. A friend of mine has a circle divided into twelve sections. There is no limit.

If you act on the ideas the pendulum gives you, you will notice a gradual improvement in every area of your life. The pendulum will also reveal your steady progress if you repeat the above experiment once a month. Gradually, areas of weakness will be overcome and this will result in benefits in every area of your life.

Many times I have seen people achieve one goal and then immediately be inspired to go out and achieve many more. A friend of mine stopped smoking and then immediately joined a public speaking club. He is now back at college completing the degree he began more than twenty years before! One success spurred him on to another and then another. You might do exactly the same.

You can draw up circles for any area of your life. My friend took up public speaking as he realized it was an area of weakness. He drew up a circle which he headed "communication." He had four quadrants labelled: public speaking, one-on-one, small groups and work. The pendulum told him that he was performing satisfactorily in every area except for public speaking.

Your circles can have as many sections as you wish. If you draw up a circle for your finances, it might contain the following sectors: wages, investments, retirement, insurance, mortgage, household expenses, vacation fund, college fund, and so on. In the process of constructing the circle, you will gain valuable insight into your earning and spending habits. The pendulum will tell you exactly where you are making progress and where you are falling back.

Let's suppose that you would like more confidence. Start by writing down as many positive things about yourself that you can. You can even include childhood successes, such as gaining a certificate for swimming twenty-five yards breast-stroke when you were ten years old. Include all your good qualities. You might like animals. If so, add it to the list.

You will probably surprise yourself with the length of this list. Now write another list of the qualities you would like to possess. Be as specific as possible. Asking for more confidence is not clear enough. We are all more confident doing some activities than we are in others. You might write down that you want to be able to converse more easily with strangers. You might want to overcome shyness, be able to speak up in a group, or be able to walk confidently into a room full of people.

Once this list is as complete as possible, think about the first item on the list. Ask your pendulum, "Would it benefit me to possess this quality?" If your pendulum gives a positive answer, ask, "Will my subconscious mind help me achieve this goal?" Sometimes your pendulum will give you a negative answer to the first question. There will be a reason for this, and it may not be to your advantage to know what it is. Usually, it is because your subconscious mind would rather have you work on one of the other qualities first. Simply move on to the next item on your list and ask the same question again.

Stop as soon as the pendulum has told you that your subconscious mind will help you. Try to put the matter right out of your mind for a few days. Then re-evaluate the situation. If you notice no change, it may be because you did not place yourself in the right environment. If your subconscious told you it would help you start conversing with strangers, it meant it, but it cannot help you if you don't find a stranger or two to talk to. You have to play your part in the exercise as well.

I remember a young relative stuttering as she made a comment at a family gathering. She had asked her subconscious to help her speak in groups. From that painful beginning she has progressed to be an excellent conversationalist in every type of situation. She had to force herself to speak at the party, and certainly played her part in the exercise. She now enjoys talking with others.

Her problem was a fear of speaking in public. We all have fears of different sorts and they can be crippling. A friend of mine had a fear of appearing foolish. Consequently, he seldom spoke for fear that he might say something that would embarrass him. A few sessions with a pendulum is starting to put him on the right track. The amazing thing is that this man has a wonderful, dry sense of humor, but only his closest friends are aware of it. To everyone else, he is a quiet person who keeps to himself.

Fear of failure is another common fear. In fact, I think most of us have experienced that fear at one time or another. Sadly, some people have it all the time. They hold themselves back by never trying anything, because they might fail.

Try writing your fears down. Your pendulum will tell you what they are if you do not already know. Now that you know what they are, you can do something about it. The best way to overcome fear is to face it. Once you have successfully faced it, you can then eliminate it from your life. You may find, like my relative, that you actually come to enjoy what you previously feared.

The pendulum can be used in all sorts of other ways for self-improvement. You can choose the right teacher, take the right course, visit the right places, and apply for the jobs that would benefit you most. You can choose the right books to read. It can even ensure that you see only the shows and movies that you will enjoy. Your dowsing skills will give you an added edge in every type of situation. Having this support will give you more self-esteem, greater confidence in all of your abilities, and put you on the right track for success.

Having access to your subconscious mind gives you an added edge which can enhance your life in many, many ways. Your pendulum can be your friend and adviser. It will show you what a wonderful miracle of creation you really are. It will also make you aware that you can achieve anything you set your mind on. Remember to aim high!

CHAPTER NINE

Agricultural Dowsing

PLANTS

Given the opportunity, dowsing can play a valuable role in agriculture. Farmers have used dowsing rods to locate water from time immemorial, but very few have ever thought of using them to choose the right crops for a certain field, or to select the right food for their animals.

Several years ago we moved to a new house. Down one side of our drive is a row of Macrocarpa trees (related to the Pine family). They make a fine display, and also make our property more private.

We were disturbed to find, shortly after moving in, that the tree nearest the road was slowly dying. We did all we could to save it, but over a period of twelve months it died.

We immediately planted another tree of the same sort in the same position. To begin with, it grew very quickly, but then during winter two years later it also died.

This was a puzzle, as the first tree had been healthy for some fifteen years before we moved in, and the other trees were all still in excellent condition.

I took samples of the soil and tested them with my pendulum. The soil taken from where the two trees had died was extremely acidic in comparison to the other samples. Obviously, this particular tree could not survive in that sort of soil.

We were curious as to how that small piece of ground had become acidic, while the soil all the other trees were growing in was alkaline. About the time we moved in, the people behind us subdivided their property and a new house was built on what had been their front yard. The property was down a long right-of-way and all the services—water, power and telephone—were buried in the ground less than two yards from our row of trees. Presumably, something in the supply of one of these had caused the soil at the bottom of our property to become acidic.

Knowing this, we were able to do something about it. The tree that is growing on the spot now is as healthy and almost as tall as the older specimens. Every now and again I check the soil with my pendulum, to ensure that it is still alkaline.

You can very easily check the soil around your home to see if it is healthy. Use your pendulum to tell you if something is wrong. Take a sample of soil, hold your pendulum over it and ask if the soil is healthy. If the answer is negative, you will have to ask further questions to find out what is wrong. The soil could be missing a trace element, for instance. By asking a series of questions you will be able to determine the problem and then ask for advice on how to correct the situation.

You can imagine how useful this can be if you are planning to buy a farm.

Your pendulum will also tell you the best place on your property for a specific plant. You can do this with map dowsing. Let's suppose you have bought a young shrub that you think will look beautiful in the middle of your front garden. Sketch a plan of your property and ask your pendulum to tell you the best place to plant it. You may find that your pendulum confirms your original idea and you can happily plant the shrub in the middle of the garden, confident that it will do well.

However, your pendulum may tell you to plant the shrub somewhere else. It may not choose a convenient place. You may have bought the shrub because it made a beautiful display, yet your pendulum tells you to plant it somewhere in the back where no one will see it! What can you do?

You could plant the shrub in the center of the garden, anyway, and hope for the best. The shrub might do well, or perhaps die, or do anything in between. However, it would not do anywhere near as well as it would have in the position the pendulum suggested. A more sensible choice would be to follow the pendulum's advice, confident that your new plant will thrive in the location suggested.

You could also ask your pendulum what would happen if you did plant the shrub in the center of the garden. The position might be satisfactory, even though it is not the best position.

Alternatively, you could ask your pendulum what needs to be done to the site you have selected to encourage the plant to grow. You can then confirm this by asking the same questions over a sample of soil taken from where you want to plant the shrub.

Suppose you have a potted plant that has been doing well, but suddenly the leaves develop a yellowish tinge. The most likely explanation is that the soil is deficient in something the plant needs. Take a sample of the soil from the pot and suspend your pendulum over it. Ask your pendulum if the soil is providing the plant with all the nutrients it requires. If you get a negative response, ask it about nutrients one at a time until you discover what is missing. At this stage you could ask the pendulum how much of the missing nutrient is required, or, alternatively, you could add small portions of the missing nutrient to the soil sample until you get a good positive response from your pendulum. By adding a proportionate amount of this nutrient to the soil in the pot, your plant will start to thrive again.

Your pendulum will also let you know what the earth thinks of changes you may be considering. Suppose you want to build an ornamental wall in your garden. Your pendulum will let you know if it is a good idea. It can also tell you where you should position it.

Suppose you have some spare land and you are wondering what to do with it. You might decide to make extra money by planting a crop of some sort to sell. Maybe your first thought is a large herb garden. Then you change your mind and think that daffodils might be a good idea. However, your partner wants to grow tomatoes and beans.

THE AUTHOR DOWSES A POTTED PLANT FOR HEALTH.

Your pendulum can solve this problem for you. First, ask if the ground is suitable for the different things you might grow. You may eliminate some, or even all, of your options with the first question. Then ask which would be the best crop for you to grow as a business. Finally, ask what, if anything, should be done to the soil before you start planting.

You can do exactly the same with animals. Should you breed cattle or sheep? Your pendulum will tell you. What about something more exotic, such as llamas? Simply ask the pendulum.

We can go even further than this. Suppose you have been successful at growing chili peppers. However, you do not want to expand further with them, as you would rather try something else for a change. What could you grow that would get on well with your chilies? Your best results will come if you plant something that harmonizes with the plants that are already there.

There are two ways of doing this. You could hold your pendulum over a chili plant and ask it if it would be happy to be in the ground next to whatever it is you have in mind. Alternatively, you could obtain a specimen of the other plant and place it about two feet away from a chili plant. Suspend your pendulum between the two and see what it does. It may gyrate (either clockwise or counter-clockwise), move two and fro between the two plants, or oscillate in the center. You can interpret these movements, according to how the pendulum reacts for you.

The late Mr. T. C. Lethbridge began an investigation into many of the trees that have passed into folklore. He discovered that many of the trees harmonized very well with humans, but others gave the opposite reaction. Interestingly, the trees that the ancient druids regarded as being supportive and protective gave a favorable response to his pendulum, while the trees that they regarded as being malevolent gave a negative response.[1]

The oak, for instance, has always been regarded as a sacred tree. The ancient druids used to gather mistletoe from it. Mr. Lethbridge found this to be a tree that reacted very favorably to his pendulum. Hazel and rowan also gave very positive responses. Elder and holly, in contrast, gave a negative reaction.

You can experiment with the trees in your locality. You will find some trees virtually reach out to you, while others hold back.

ANIMALS

Your dowsing skills can be extremely useful in dealing with animals. Unfortunately, animals cannot tell us what is wrong with them when they are ill. There are occasional exceptions. Years ago we had a Labrador dog who took himself to the veterinarian whenever he felt ill, so he was certainly able to let us know! This is unusual, though. Fortunately, we can use our pendulum to determine whatever the problem may be with our pet.

Suppose you have a dog that is noticeably unwell. Hold your pendulum over your pet and ask if the problem is a major one. Naturally, if the illness is serious you will want to get your pet to a veterinarian as quickly as possible. You may want to ask your pendulum if the dog should be taken to a veterinary clinic.

You can assist the veterinarian by locating the cause of the illness. Your pendulum will let you know if the problem is in the liver, for instance.

Assuming the problem is not a major one, we can ask the pendulum what we can do to help the animal. What would be the best course of treatment? Often, with animals, sleep is the best medicine. The pendulum may suggest the best food or food supplement to help the dog recover as quickly as possible.

You can also test your dog at other times to see if he or she is in good health. If the pendulum decides your dog is not well, you can then do something about it at a very early stage, rather than waiting for the problem to become obvious.

Your pendulum can be very useful in determining the best foods for your animals. Your dog might adore two commercial brands of dog food. The pendulum can tell you which one is the better for your dog. Interestingly enough, if you own two dogs, you might find that while one brand is better for one dog, the

EVEN YOUR PETS, SUCH AS THIS CAT, CAN BE DOWSED FOR HEALTH.

other brand is better for the other! We had this situation occur with our two cats.

Animals need exercise. Ask your pendulum if your pet is getting sufficient exercise. Sometimes this is very obvious, particularly if your pet is getting obese. However, at times you may feel you are giving your pet plenty of exercise when, in fact, he or she needs more.

Our neighbors own a beautiful German Shepherd dog. They look after him very well and take him for lengthy walks every morning and evening. Despite this, they were always taking him to the veterinarian for all sorts of small problems. I offered to help. With their permission I asked my pendulum a number of questions about their dog and was told that he was not getting enough exercise. Nowadays, as a result of this, one of the owners' sons comes home and takes it for an additional walk in the middle of the day. The dog has not needed medical attention since.

Naturally, the pendulum can also be used with large numbers of animals. If you are a farmer you can ask your pendulum if a certain field is right for your animals. You can ask if the necessary nutrients can be obtained from the soil. You can find out if any radiation is being caused by overhead power lines or underground streams that might affect the health of your animals.

There are many documented cases of animals behaving strangely when there is a buildup of atmospheric electricity. In May 1876, there was a major earthquake in Northern Italy. In the days leading up to it, people noticed wild deer coming down from the hills. Cats left home, dogs barked, and even rats and mice were out in the open in broad daylight.[2] The earthquake, when it came, was a total surprise for the people, but the animals had known about it for days beforehand. Animals are much more aware of vibrations than we think. Some people claim that the tusks and horns of many animals actually serve as dowsing devices, enabling them to find water when they need it.

Many years ago I read a newspaper article about a farmer who was able to check on his animals, even in the middle of a major storm, from the comfort of his living room. He would ask his pendulum questions while the storm raged outside. If the pendulum told him that something was wrong with his livestock, he would go and attend to them. One night, according to the article, he was checking up on his animals before going to bed and the pendulum alerted him to a problem. He went to investigate and found rustlers on his property. Thanks to his pendulum, none of the animals were stolen.

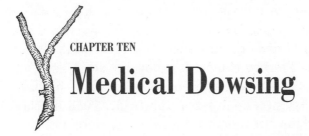

CHAPTER TEN

Medical Dowsing

Early in this century it occurred to Abbé Alexis Mermet that as his pendulum was so accurate in finding water and oil underground, it might also be able to pick up vibrations from the human body. He likened the veins and arteries to underwater streams. He made experiments and found, to his surprise, that he could. Not only was he able to determine areas of illness and disease, but his pendulum was also able to recommend effective treatment. He concluded that the pendulum was picking up changes in the energy fields of his patients. In 1930, another priest, the Abbé Alexis Bouly, called this discovery "radiesthesia," which means "perceiving radiations." Abbé Bouly was ultimately awarded the Legion of Honor for his work in dowsing for microbes.

There have always been healers who could cure by the laying-on of hands. The Bible records Jesus Christ healing in this manner. These healers are, in a sense, dowsers as they can often detect the exact site of the illness through the sensations they receive in their hands.

The earth's radiations have a profound effect upon us, even though we are usually quite unaware of them. Georges Lakhovsky was able to demonstrate that the geological nature of the soil played a large role in the incidence of cancers. He concluded that soils that absorbed external radiations, such as sand, sandstone and gravel, were associated with the least amount of cancers. Impermeable soils, such as clay, carboniferous strata and mineral ores, were associated with the highest incidences of cancer.[1]

Obviously, the terrain is only one factor in the causes of cancer, but most researchers feel that harmful earth radiations play a major role in a number of illnesses. These include: sterility, rheumatism, arthritis, tuberculosis, lumbago, goiter, headaches, fibrositis, insomnia, chronic fatigue, and some types of asthma.[2]

Earth rays have long been known to affect animals as well as humans. It was known that sheep do not like them, for instance, and consequently sheep were often put on potential building sites to see where they slept. Anywhere that sheep lay down to sleep was considered a safe place to build a house. Dogs, horses, cows, pigs, and mice also tend to avoid these rays, but cats, bees, and ants like them.

Trees can also be divided into two groups. Oaks, firs, plums, cherries and peaches all thrive on earth rays. Apples, pears, beeches, ashes, and all nut-bearing trees avoid them.

Asparagus, mushrooms, mistletoes and many herbs are examples of plants that seek the rays.

Roses, sunflowers, lilies, azaleas, cucumbers, celery, and onions all avoid them.

Many methods have been tried to eliminate the effects of these harmful radiations. Georges Lakhovsky devised the Lakhovsky loop, which consists of loops of wire tied around the frame of beds. Another method is to drive specially prepared copper coils into the ground directly over the water courses as they enter and leave the house.[3]

In the 1930s, Pierre Cody, a French engineer, decided to investigate houses where people had died of cancer. Using an electroscope, he discovered that the air in the houses where the victims had died contained a high level of radon, an extremely deadly gas.[4] From this small beginning, researchers have carried on more and more research into earth radiation. In both the United States and Great Britain, national surveys were done of the radon level in people's homes. The results were alarming. Thousands of homes were affected, and the results indicated that, in the United States, one home in every eight was contaminated.[5]

Incidentally, radioactivity can sometimes affect the dowsing response as well. Many of the British army officers who dowsed in India in the first half of this century discovered something they called "the Deccan Trap." This is a stratum of mildly radioactive rock which affected the dowsing instruments and produced strange results.[6]

As well as radiations from the earth, we are also exposed daily to radiations of all sorts—microwaves, television sets, radios, computers, etc. These EMFs (electro-magnetic fields) are becoming more and more worrisome as our use of technology increases. Twenty-five years ago the average house contained a color television, a stereo unit and a transistor radio. Compare that with today.

Our office environments have changed dramatically as well. Computers, disc drives and other peripherals, photocopiers, laser printers, fax modems, and the proliferation of power cables mean that every office worker is exposed to EMFs on a daily basis. A 1993 survey by USA Weekend magazine showed that thirty-five percent of the respondents considered EMFs to be the main health environment priority. Workers are starting to question the safety of their work environments and this has created a whole new market for dowsers.

Some scientists still claim that the health risks are negligible. However, other studies show likely links to Alzheimer's Disease, Amyotrophic Lateral Sclerosis, a variety of cancers, miscarriages, depression, headaches, and chronic fatigue. The human immune system is also suppressed by continued exposure to EMFs.

No one knows what constitutes a safe level of exposure. Avoidance, wherever possible, is the only sensible policy. In this technological age, complete avoidance is impossible and unrealistic, but there are things we can do to reduce our exposure.

We can test our homes with a pendulum to see if any harmful radiation is affecting us. We can change the positions of possessions, such as a television set, to eliminate negative influences. Try moving items such as this around and then test them again, until your pendulum gives you a positive response.

It is not so easy with harmful radiations from the earth. I would recommend that you move house if you discover that these are present. Even if your health is not being affected by these at the moment, why put yourself in a potentially dangerous situation?

Geobiologists believe that there is a network of grids of radiation that covers the entire earth. They are able to sense these grids by dowsing, and claim to treat illnesses by moving the patients' beds away from these grids. Personally, I would rather move out of the house.

Test your house by walking around it with your dowsing instrument. Then check each room in turn. If your house is more than one story high, any rays found on a bottom level will be repeated in the upper lovels. Abbé Mermet insisted that it did not matter how many floors there were in the building. Even on the tenth floor, for instance, a person can be exposed to harmful radiations.

The strength of the rays varies according to the time of day. Their intensity increases in the evening and is at its strongest between one and two A.M. At the time of the full moon they are some three times stronger than at other times.[7] Do not conduct a test during stormy weather, as the radiation is extremely strong and potentially dangerous at these times. After testing your home for radiation, take a bath or shower.

Underground streams have been linked to such illnesses as insomnia, rheumatism, arthritis, and cancer. Most animals avoid areas with subterranean streams. When penned or housed over such an area, they will always sleep in the unaffected parts and tend to avoid the areas above underground water. This underground water creates what is known as telluric radiation. If a number of these streams cross each other, the harmful effects are magnified.

The famous Australian dowser Evelyn Penrose said that she experienced a "sickening, unhealthy feeling" when she sensed telluric radiation.[8]

Ralph Whitlock, author of *Water Divining and Other Dowsing*, experienced telluric radiation in his home. His wife had been sleeping badly and experiencing nightmares. As an experiment, they changed places in the bed. She immediately began sleeping better, but both of them experienced disturbing dreams. Ralph Whitlock dowsed the bedroom and found an underwater stream that went beneath his wife's side of the bed. They moved the bed to the other side of the room, and now both of them sleep soundly and peacefully.[9]

In 1976, Herbert Douglas, a Vermont businessman, using a plastic dowsing rod, dowsed the bedrooms of fifty-five people suffering from arthritis. He was not surprised to find that every one of them was sleeping over a vein of underground water. He suggested that they change their sleeping place, and without exception everyone experienced reduction of pain and even total disappearance of pain.[10]

In the late 1970s, Jacob Stängle, a German engineer, invented a machine to record these radiations. As it passes over an area where radiation is present, a moving pen records the level. Some forty years earlier, in 1929, a survey of cancer deaths in the small town of Vilsbiburg showed that a significant proportion of the victims lived in houses over radiation zones. Stängle was invited to test his machine in this town. Not surprisingly, the graphs produced by his machine were identical to the results obtained by dowsing in the 1929 survey.[11]

Not long ago, I attended a meeting of a dowsing society, and the lecturer was giving us a demonstration of his use of the pendulum. As he moved to his right, the pendulum suddenly stopped its movement. Sure enough, radiation was coming from a power socket nearby. The lecturer was able to measure the level of radiation with other instruments, but it was interesting to see the pendulum react dramatically in the middle of a demonstration of something else entirely!

You can do a simple pendulum experiment yourself. Hold the pendulum over your thigh and watch it give a response. Now, sharply slap this thigh with your free hand and you will see the pendulum give a totally different response. If you keep your pendulum in position, it will eventually start giving the response for healthy tissue once again, indicating that your thigh has recovered from the slap.

Since Abbé Mermet's amazing discovery, "pendular diagnosis" has become an extremely popular method of alternative health care. A pendulum is a standard item of medical equipment for doctors in many parts of Europe, particularly in France. Mermet, himself, taught his method to doctors, herbalists, veterinarians, and other priests. The amount of good he did with this discovery is incalculable. Abbé

Kunzle, a renowned healer, learned Mermet's method and used it after World War I, when influenza swept across Europe killing thousands. In Kunzle's own parish, not a single person died.[12]

METHODS OF DIAGNOSIS

Before you use your dowsing skills for health purposes, make sure that it is legal for you to do so. Unless you have medical qualifications, in many parts of the world it is illegal to diagnose illnesses.

The simplest method of diagnosis is to have the person who is suffering from a health problem with you. Ask the patient to lie down on his or her back and hold your pendulum over the area of the head. The pendulum will start to move. In my case, it is a clockwise gyration. Your pendulum may give you a different response. There is no need to think of anything. Simply move the pendulum slowly over every part of the body. If the person is healthy, your pendulum will continue with its initial movement. However, if something is wrong with the body, the pendulum will react when you are holding it over the affected part.

General J. Scott Elliot describes his first attempt at medical dowsing in his book *Dowsing: One Man's Way*. He had been trying to convince a group of archaeologists of the reality of dowsing, with no success. As he was leaving, one of the archaeologists removed his jacket and asked the general if he could find a piece of shrapnel in his back. Even though he had never attempted this type of dowsing before, Scott Elliot agreed to try. It took him just three seconds to locate it.[13]

Abbé Mermet worked with patients in the same way he did his map dowsing. His pendulum was held away from the patient and he used the first finger of his other hand as a pointer. As he moved this pointer over the body, his pendulum would gyrate over healthy organs and oscillate over unhealthy ones.[14]

One of the most remarkable discoveries of pendulum diagnosis is that it can give advance warning of an illness. Suppose you are testing a friend and find that the pendulum changes direction over her stomach. She may insist that there is nothing wrong, but in time, you will be proven correct. When this sort of thing happens, I always suggest that the person have a medical checkup.

This leads us to an interesting question. If we perform this diagnosis and see that someone is about to get a cold, and, because the person is forewarned he or she is able to ward off the cold, how can we prove that we successfully prevented it?

We can also diagnose someone who is not in our presence. Make a representative drawing of the person you wish to diagnose (See Figure 10A). It doesn't have to be exact. Write the person's name above it, to identify it as representing him or her.

Then suspend your pendulum over every area of the drawing. If it reacts over a certain part, we know the general area where the problem is, but we need to be much more precise than that. You will need to have access to a book on anatomy. I find *The Anatomy Coloring Book*[15] useful for this. Using this book, ask the pendulum about each organ, one at a time. Once you have identified the affected organ, you can

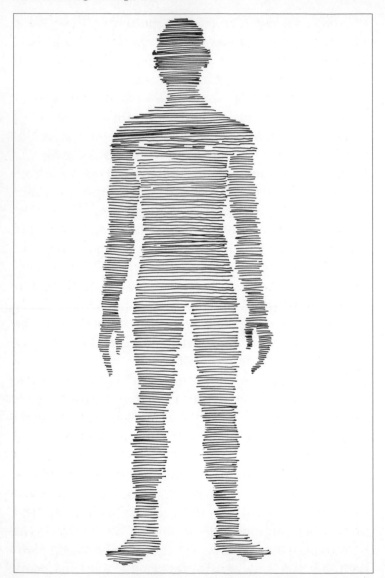

Figure 10A: This can be used as a representation of the person from whom you wish to do a diagnosis.

ask further questions to determine exactly what is wrong and what would be the best form of treatment. I always ask, "Should this person see a doctor about this problem?"

Most radiesthetists find it helpful to hold a sample from the patient in their free hand. This could be a small vial containing a sample of urine, a lock of hair, specimen of blood or saliva, etc. Experiment with and without these samples (often referred to as "witnesses"). Bear in mind that it may not always be possible to have a sample, particularly if the person is many miles away. If you can, learn how to diagnose without the need for a sample.

Instead of a drawing, you may prefer to use a photograph of the person. Suspend your pendulum over the photograph and ask, "Is this person in good health?" If the pendulum gives a negative answer, you can proceed to ask more and more questions until you determine what the problem is.

The author of *Diagnostic Analysis with a Pendulum*[16] is a doctor who prefers to remain anonymous. He describes how he diagnoses a patient using his pendulum and a small sample of blood. He begins by using an iris-diagnosis chart. In fact, he recommends using charts for everything. That way, nothing is accidentally missed. The iris-diagnosis chart lists the nine main systems of the body, and enables him to quickly determine where the patient's problems lie. He holds the pendulum in one hand and uses a pointer in the other. As he slowly moves the pointer, he observes the movements of the pendulum. In this way, he is also able to calculate many of the laboratory figures, such as the pH of the blood, urine, saliva, spinal fluid, etc. He then determines the correct diet for the patient, along with homeopathic medications.

The blood sample also tells him if and where the patient might need a spinal manipulation or physiotherapy. If the patient is lying down on the examination table, he will hold the pendulum over the person's spine. The pendulum will simply move back and forth along the path of the spine when everything is normal. However, when it finds a subluxation or other abnormality, the pendulum will move at a right angle to its original path. When this happens, he holds the pendulum on each side of the vertebrae to determine which side the problem is on.

Once the spinal problem has been identified, it is usually a simple matter for an osteopath or chiropractor to correct it.

Body, Mind, and Spirit

The pendulum is not able to separate our physical self from our mental and spiritual selves. Consequently, it can be used to diagnose mental and spiritual illnesses. It can trace the causes and suggest a suitable treatment. As most illnesses are caused by mental and spiritual stress, radiesthesia and radionics are the only ways to diagnose these types of disease. Most doctors around the world still concentrate on the symptoms and ignore the underlying cause. Even doctors who take psychology into account are still ignoring the spiritual side of our beings. Fortunately, the pendulum can measure the body, mind, and spirit.

Ideally, all three of these should be in balance and in harmony with each other. People with this arrangement are healthy and enjoy life.

THE SUBTLE BODIES

Psychics have been aware of our subtle bodies for thousands of years. Even though these bodies that surround us like a cocoon are invisible, they are nonetheless extremely important in keeping us mentally, emotionally, and spiritually well. The etheric body provides energy and the life force to our physical bodies. The emotional body expresses and responds to our emotions. The mental body contains our mind and enables us to think. A blockage in any of these subtle bodies can create illness in the physical body.

Fortunately, we can easily test the health of the subtle bodies with our pendulums.

Ask the person being tested to lie on his or her stomach. Suspend your pendulum over the center of the person's back, and ask, either out loud or to yourself, "Is this person's etheric body healthy?"

Follow this by asking about the person's mental, emotional, and physical bodies.

It is unusual for all four bodies to be in perfect health. If three of the four are in good shape, the person is regarded as being healthy. Two out of four is considered average. If just one out of the four is positive, the person is overdue for a restful vacation. If none of the four is positive, the person is well on the way to a breakdown and needs to do something to correct the situation right away.

The physical body is healed by doing whatever the person's health professional recommends.

The etheric body is healed with plenty of fresh air, moderate exercise, sufficient rest, and deep breathing.

The emotional body is healed with creative activity. Many people claim they have no time for a creative outlet, but they need to make the time if their emotional body is out of balance. This body can also be helped with pleasant music, happy surroundings, agreeable companions, and fresh air.

The mental body is healed with positive affirmations. Disease in the mental body is caused by too many negative thoughts. Few of us stop to think how many of our thoughts each day are positive, and how many are negative. With most people, the negative far outweighs the positive. Affirmations are an excellent method of bringing our mental bodies back into balance.

The Chakras

The seven chakras are energy centers that communicate between the physical and subtle bodies. They are subject to blockages and over- and under-stimulation. Negative emotions affect them, and consequently our chakras reveal information about the stresses, strains, and conflicts we all experience. We can read the level of these tensions with a pendulum and then restore the chakras, healing and providing the person with emotional balance once again.

The three lower chakras relate to the person's will. The sacral chakra represents the person's willpower and life force. The navel chakra represents the person's emotional desires. The solar plexus chakra represents the person's intellect and communication center.

Most of us spend a great deal of time trying to handle and cope with these particular energies, at the expense of the other four chakras. Unfortunately, the higher chakras can only work effectively if the lower ones are in balance. And it is the higher chakras that have access to the subtle bodies.

The heart chakra is concerned with idealism and love. The throat chakra is related to creativity and responsibility. The brow chakra is concerned with leadership and personal magnetism. The crown chakra is concerned with service and intuition.

It is a simple matter to test the freedom of the chakras using our pendulum. Have the person lie on his or her back and suspend the pendulum over each chakra in turn. The chakras are all powerful energy centers and should send the pendulum gyrating in a clockwise direction.

If the pendulum moves in any other direction, be it from side to side, to and fro, or counter-clockwise, something is out of balance.

It is possible for a chakra to be temporarily out of balance. As these powerful energy centers are ruled by our emotions, a temporary upset will affect them. If someone loses his temper before having his chakras tested, at least one of his chakras will be temporarily imbalanced. However, as he calms down, the chakra will restore itself.

However, there are also many cases where the chakra is permanently out of balance. Whatever emotional stress caused the situation in the first place has not been relieved and the person could be suffering physical problems as a result.

We restore the chakra balance by a process known as "winding." This is done by holding your hand palm down about six inches from the chakra and making several circular passes in a clockwise direction. It makes no difference which hand you use.[17]

GENERAL WELL-BEING

The pendulum can help us make the right decisions for general physical well-being. For instance, if you are lacking in energy and vitality, the pendulum will be able to tell you what is causing it and what dietary supplements would be beneficial to restore you to good health.

A pendulum with about four and a half inches of thread is ideal for this sort of thing. However, you may wish to have your pendulum in harmony with the items you are testing. You do this by suspending your pendulum over the item you are testing and gradually let more and more thread run through your fingers until the pendulum starts gyrating. Now suspend the still gyrating pendulum over the palm of your free hand. If the gyrations continue as strongly as they did over the tested item, it is safe for you to take the item in moderation.

Suppose you had a headache and were thinking of taking some aspirin. It might pay to test the aspirin with your pendulum by asking, "Is an aspirin beneficial for me at this time?" The answer might be "no." When this occurs, ask more questions. Maybe a walk in the fresh air will be sufficient to cure your headache.

I have a friend who is highly allergic to monosodium glutamate (MSG) that is put into many foods to enhance the flavor. Unfortunately, she gets violently ill after eating it and has been admitted to hospitals several times due to the MSG in her food. Consequently, she is extremely careful with what she eats. All the same, every now and again, she gets caught out when MSG is added to a food where she did not expect to find it.

She now carries a pendulum with her everywhere she goes, and suspends it over her food before eating it, asking, "Is their any MSG on this plate?" Since doing this she has had no problems. On several occasions the pendulum has alerted her to the presence of MSG and she has been able to avoid the food.

This is making highly practical use of the pendulum to preserve her physical well-being. You can do the same with food that you suspect may not be good for your system. Try it with chocolate and see what your pendulum tells you!

ABSENT HEALING

We have already seen how a good dowser can determine the health of people and animals who may be far away. The dowser can even ask his or her pendulum to suggest the right cure. This seems to be further evidence of the psychic hypothesis about dowsing.

I know a lady who uses a pendulum to determine health problems of people who might be hundreds of miles away. She prefers to do this with a photograph of the person in front of her, but she can also do it from the person's name. Once she has determined the problem, she sends healing thoughts to the person. She is in great demand because of the success of her absent healing.

A few years ago this might have been considered far-fetched, but scientists are proving that healing thoughts are beneficial, even over long distances. Experiments have been conducted that show how healing thoughts positively affect high blood pressure, heart attacks, wounds of all sorts, headaches and anxiety.[18] It makes no difference how far away the person is. You can send healing thoughts to someone in the same room as you, or to someone halfway around the world, and be able to help them equally.

No one has a right to intrude on you, and naturally, you have no right to intrude on anyone else. Many people enjoy their illnesses. It may be satisfying something that was previously lacking in their lives—attention, perhaps. Do not try and heal someone who has not asked for it.

Do not try to diagnose and heal yourself. You already know how easy it is to influence the pendulum using your mind. If you feel you may have such-and-such illness, your subconscious mind could make the pendulum confirm this when, in fact, you may be perfectly healthy or be suffering from something else entirely.

Try and confirm all your findings by other means, whenever possible. After all, you may be wrong. In fact, when you first start, you are likely to be wrong much of the time. Do not become discouraged by your failures, though. The more practice you put in, the better you will become.

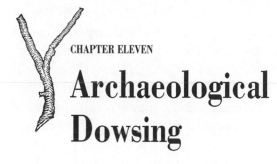

CHAPTER ELEVEN

Archaeological Dowsing

If you can successfully dowse for water, oil, and minerals underground, it is not that big a step to also dowse for artifacts from the past. There have been many instances where archaeological dowsers have discovered items and information that could not have been found in any other way.

A notable example of this was an archaeological survey of the battlefield at Borodino, the site of a particularly brutal battle between Napoleon's troops and the Russians in 1812. Maps made at the time were found to be extremely unreliable, and the terrain has changed markedly over the years. Roads have been built, forests grown, and a second battle occurred on the site during the second World War.

Despite all of this, Alexander Pluzhnikov was able to detect a large number of military excavations as well as graves of Russian and French soldiers. Of particular importance was his ability at locating the "wolf holes," holes drilled into the ground to break the legs of the enemies' horses. These holes had long since been filled in and even plowed over, making them impossible to locate by any other method.[1]

In his book *Dowsing: One Man's Way*, retired general Jim Scott Elliot describes his first experiences at archaeological dowsing. He began by locating a forgotten underground water tank halfway up a hill behind his house in Scotland. Later, a farmer told him that a small black patch appeared in a field of his whenever it was plowed. General Scott Elliot dowsed the area and discovered something unusual under the surface. Excavations were made which revealed an early Bronze Age fire pit. Encouraged by these initial successes, Scott Elliot continued and eventually located a large site at Chieveley, Berkshire. Excavations unearthed Roman Punic remains from the first century. No one was aware of these remains until General Scott Elliot map-dowsed the area with his pendulum.[2]

Some people regard archaeological dowsing as being so commonplace that it hardly deserves mention. T. C. Lethbridge mentions his discovery of an Anglo-Saxon cemetery in this way in his book *The Power of the Pendulum*.[3] In the 1920s, Maria Mattaloni, a twenty-four-year-old peasant girl, successfully dowsed for Etruscan tombs at Capena, close to Rome. She also took her dowsing skills for granted.[4]

A friend of mine in New Zealand dowses for ancient Maori and Moriori pa sites in the same way. These ancient settlements were often only temporary homes and virtually all trace of them has disappeared, apart from bones, shells, and other refuse from their food. My friend was dowsing for greenstone (a type of jade) when he unexpectedly came across the site of an ancient village. Unfortunately, archaeologists have been skeptical and he has not yet been able to prove his findings.

Not all archaeologists are skeptical, fortunately. Simple intuition led J. J. Winkelmann to the treasures of Pompeii and Herculaneum in the eighteenth century. In 1845, intuition led Henry Layard to the site of Nimrud and to Sennacherib's huge library of tablets at Ninevah. In 1871, Heinrich Schliemann found the site of ancient Troy with little more than his intuition and a copy of *The Iliad*.

Norman Emerson asked psychics to dowse over maps of the Montreal River in Ontario. In just one day they indicated thirty-two Indian sites. Emerson's colleagues had spent the previous five years unsuccessfully surveying the same area.[5]

William Ross and William Noble, both archaeologists at McMasters University in Canada, have experienced remarkable successes in map dowsing by holding an arrowhead over a map of a previously unexplored area.[6]

For the last fifteen years Denis Briggs, a retired engineer, has astounded the archaeological community in Great Britain with his ability at locating the remains of ancient churches. He uses a pair of angle rods to determine the positions of underground remains. He began by drawing up plans of local churches which he showed to Professor Richard Bailey, an authority on church archaeology. These plans showed not only the positions of existing church walls, but also the positions of the original ones.

Professor Bailey was skeptical, but agreed to a series of tests. Some of these were failures and others were inconclusive, but seven of the thirteen tests were regarded by Professor Bailey as being successful. His conclusion was that archaeologists should add dowsing to their arsenal as it appeared to work.[6] Naturally, his ideas were condemned by many, but he gained support from several academics, including Professor Philip Rahtz, emeritus professor of archaeology at the University of York. Professor Bailey, Eric Cambridge, an archaeological colleague, and Denis Briggs ultimately wrote a book about their experiences, called *Dowsing and Church Archaeology*.[8]

One of Denis Briggs' successes was his survey of St. John's Church in Newcastle-upon-Tyne. In 1982, Denis Briggs divined that a linear feature would be found running across the north aisle of this medieval church. Three years later, archaeologists found a slot in the clay under the church at exactly the position indicated by Briggs. This may well have held an ancient foundation.[9]

Dowsers and psychics have known for years that many ancient churches were built directly over lines of geodetic energy. Similar lines have been located by dowsers at Stonehenge and other megalithic sites. Guy Underwood, in his book *The Pattern of the Past*,[10] suggests that certain parts of ecclesiastical buildings have their own special characteristics that can be measured. For example, he says that north and south porches and doors were always found on transverse lines, and the naves and chancels were always on geodetic lines. This means that these sites, virtually all of them venerated as spiritual places long before Christian times, were chosen by people who were well aware of their special power and energy.

Additionally, springs of water are usually found at these sacred places, not only in Europe but in most parts of Asia as well. The lines of energy have been described as possessing yang (masculine) energy, while the springs of water possess yin (feminine) energy.[11]

You can do archaeological dowsing anywhere in the world by using maps and your pendulum. It makes more sense to start with maps of areas close to you, as you can then verify your findings on the site. Decide what it is you are specifically looking for. You may be looking for sites of a certain period or of a certain race of people. For instance, if you live in Britain you may wish to dowse for Roman remains. Think about what you are divining for as you dowse over the maps. This prevents you from locating other remains that are not of interest to you. On the other hand, if you are searching for ancient remains of any sort, keep that in mind, and your pendulum will locate them for you.

Once you find a site, you will have to visit it and dowse over the area to confirm your findings and to outline the area. In practice, I have always found farmers very obliging and interested in what might lie underneath their ground. They are usually happy for you to dig and see what you can find. I have not experienced the same cooperation in cities.

Probably the best way to gain experience in archaeological dowsing is to visit a suitable site and ask the archaeologists for permission to dowse. If you are turned down, find another dig and ask again. Treat the archaeologists and their work with respect and conduct yourself professionally at all times. You may well be able to help each other.

Alternatively, you can check out old historical records of your locality and then dowse for the positions of buildings and other items mentioned. Report your findings to archaeologists, historical societies, and other people who may be interested. Be prepared for some skepticism, but also be persistent so that your dowsing can be proved, one way or the other.

One wonderful aspect of archaeological dowsing is that no damage is done to the environment or to the artifacts being dowsed for. Most archaeological dowsing starts with map dowsing. Then, once you have located a suitable place, all you need do is walk over the area with your dowsing rod. Your rod will also tell you the exact dimensions of the underground object. For instance, if an object is found in a remote field, you can dowse the area and determine what else is buried below the surface. It could be a few small objects, a buried building, or even an entire town.

It is also a considerable time-saver. Archaeologists could spend months minutely examining an area which you could dowse in an hour or two. Naturally, once you have located something, excavation will need to be done, but you will know exactly where to dig. You will quickly become an expert with a spade once you take up archaeological dowsing!

The most important aspect in archaeological dowsing is to have a clear picture in your mind of what you are looking for. If you are map-dowsing to try to find dinosaur bones, for example, your pendulum will not react at all when it is over an ancient buried village. The more specific you are, the more successful you will be.

Learn as much as you can about archaeology as well, if you plan to do this sort of dowsing seriously. The more knowledge you have, the more successful you will become.

CHAPTER TWELVE

Psychic Dowsing

We are all psychic, even though not everyone likes the term. We all have the ability to enter a room where two people have been arguing and instantly feel the change in atmosphere. The expression, "I could have cut the air with a knife," applies to this feeling. Likewise, most people have suddenly become aware that someone was staring at them, even if the other person was behind them. We have all met people and felt instantly that they could not be trusted.

Less common, but still frequently found, are people who have experienced premonitions in the form of dreams. *Déjà vu*, the feeling of being somewhere before, is also common.

All of these experiences are perfectly natural examples of our psychic sensibilities at work. They are so commonplace that we take them for granted. Dowsers are particularly tuned into their environment and it is not surprising to learn that Verne Cameron, the famous dowser from California, was able to pick up people's thoughts with his "aurameter."[1]

Naturally, it takes considerable practice to get to that level, but you will be surprised at how easy it can be to pick up impressions of what other people are thinking. In one sense, all dowsing is an example of clairvoyance, as we are finding things that are unknown to us or to anyone else.

T. C. Lethbridge measured people's psychic potentials with his pendulum and found vast differences with a cross-section of people. He also found that everyone's potential varied depending on their health and emotional state. According to him, most people were in a range from zero to fifty, but a few people actually had negative psychic potential. He described these people as "vampires," drawing energy away from others. If you have ever been in the company of someone who left you feeling drained and exhausted, you will have met one of these "vampires."[2] Fortunately, there are not too many of them around.

I have found that skeptics often have the same draining effect. For many years, I did home psychic parties and it was always easy to tell if there was a skeptic in the room, as my results were never as good. Incidentally, after one of those parties, a skeptic came up to me and booked a party for her friends. She had been impressed with what I had done, even though I had not been very happy myself. At her party, my results were much better, and this must have been because she was no longer skeptical, or was at least willing to suspend disbelief.

T. C. Lethbridge was one scientist who accepted the psychic world as being real. Other scientists have also looked at dowsing from a psychic perspective. Possibly the most notable of these was Solco Tromp, a professor of geology. For several years he conducted exhaustive tests at Leiden University in the Netherlands. He also explored as much previous research that he could find. In 1949, he published his findings in a 534-page book called *Psychical Physics*.[3] Tromp believed that parapsychologists, doctors, and physicists would have to work together in harmony to explain the reality of dowsing. He doubted that this would ever happen, as he considered most scientists to be lacking in courage and insight. Virtually nothing has changed in this regard since Tromp's book was published. Even in the Soviet Union, where dowsing is regarded highly, some scientists still refuse to accept it, because they say it is related to parapsychology, and therefore must be fraudulent.[4]

Map dowsing with a pendulum could be considered as a psychic activity. A scientist friend of mine uses map dowsing as his main argument for not accepting the reality of dowsing. "How can it be possible for someone to sit down in New Jersey with a map and tell me where to find water in Outer Mongolia?" he growls. "It's just psychic mumbo-jumbo!" I've suggested that he try it himself, or at least put a good dowser to the test. He refuses to do this. He also conveniently overlooks the fact the map dowsers get good results. I have not dared tell him about dowsers who are able to diagnose patients who are hundreds of miles away, or detect diseases by suspending a pendulum over a photograph.

Many psychics use pendulums in their work.[5] The pendulum makes a particularly good tool to use in developing psychic potential. Here are some experiments that you can try with a partner and a pendulum. You may also like to try them using a single angle rod.

READ MY MIND

Sit behind your friend, so you cannot unconsciously read the changing expressions on his or her face. Start by asking out loud questions for which you already know the answers. For instance, you might say, "Are you forty-two years old?" Your friend is not to say anything, but has to think "yes," or "no." You will find your pendulum will start moving in the right direction to indicate the correct answer.

After your pendulum has given the correct answer to three or four of these questions, it is time to start asking questions that you do not know the answers to. Your friend has to think "yes," "no," or "I don't want to answer," to each question.

Do not tell your friend what the pendulum is saying, but keep a record of each answer. After four or five questions, show the results to your friend and see how well your pendulum has done.

MIND-READING BY NUMBERS

Again, place your friend in front of you and ask him or her to think of any single digit number. Ask the pendulum, "Is my friend thinking of number one? Number two?" Carry on until you reach number nine. The pendulum will give you a different response to one of the numbers. Check to see if your friend was thinking of this number.

Many people find it difficult to concentrate on one number for the length of time it takes to perform this test. If this is the case, have your friend write down the number and keep looking at it for the duration of the experiment.

PENDULUM GRAPHOLOGY

Ask a friend to collect several samples of people's handwriting, preferably of people you do not know. Spread the samples in a row in front of you. Have your friend write down the first names of each person on small pieces of paper.

Let's imagine that the first name is Chuck. Hold the pendulum over the first sample and ask "Did Chuck write this letter?" Do this over each sample in turn. Your pendulum should give a positive response over one sample. Place the piece of paper with the name Chuck on it beneath this sample.

Continue the exercise with each of the other names in turn. If the second name was Betty, hold the pendulum over each sample in turn, even the one that you think was written by Chuck.

Hopefully, at the end you will have one name beneath each sample. Ask your friend to let you know how well you did.

The best way to succeed with this experiment is to ignore the handwriting completely and simply trust the pendulum to give you the correct answer. As soon as you start looking at the handwriting, your mind will immediately start forming conclusions that may not be correct.

WHERE IN THE HOUSE

Ask your friend to stand or sit in any room of his or her house. You can be anywhere else in the world, as long as you know what rooms your friend has. Ask your pendulum "Is my friend in the living room?" "How about the master bedroom?" "The kitchen?" Go through the entire house and then see if your pendulum has given you the correct answer.

Some people find it easier to do this by holding their pendulum over a plan of their friend's home.

WHERE IN THE WORLD

For this test you will need two atlases, preferably identical. Have your friend sit in one room and select any page in the atlas. He or she has to concentrate on that page. Sit down in another room and hold your pendulum over each page in turn, asking if each one is the correct one. When your pendulum tells you that you are looking at the right page, check it with your friend.

With large books the process can be speeded up by asking your pendulum questions before you even open the atlas. Ask, "Is the page in the first fifty pages of the book?" If you get a positive answer, ask, "Is it one of the first forty pages?" You will gradually pinpoint the correct page, and then it is a simple matter to open the book to that page and ask the pendulum, "Is this the correct page?"

Do not expect miracles the first time you try these experiments. Make sure you choose a partner who shares your interest in the subject. Your results will be better if you take the tests in a spirit of fun. A grim determination to succeed always produces adverse results. Do not spend too much time on each session. Once you get tired or bored, your results will drop quickly. Twenty minutes two or three times a week is better than one hour once a week. Your initial results are likely to be mixed, but you will notice a gradual improvement as you practice.

CHAPTER THIRTEEN

Controversial Rays

Over the years I have met many people who discovered they could dowse, but later gave it up after studying the subject further. This is a sad situation that seems to indicate that often "ignorance is bliss" when it comes to dowsing. Doubtless, this is why many uneducated people are so successful at it. They do not think about it, or question it; they simply do it.

When I become interested in a subject, I want to know as much as possible about it, and dowsing was no exception. I read everything I could find, and, like many other interested people, became bogged down in much of the information about "rays" and "serial numbers." There is no doubt in my mind that the rays and serial numbers help many people with their dowsing work, but unfortunately, they are also responsible for turning people away from the subject.

Many successful dowsers use the rays all the time and implicitly believe in them. Many others, just as successful, deny that they exist.

Abbé Mermet was the first to discover these rays. He noticed that every object in the universe has what he called a "fundamental ray" that moves away from the object in a specific angle to the north-south axis (See Figure 13A). This ray is believed to be a narrow field of radiation limited in height, breadth, and length. The fundamental ray is of major importance in healing with radionics, as the fundamental ray is linked with the patient.

In his experiments, Abbé Mermet noticed that silver coins have a fundamental ray which heads in an easterly direction. Copper coins, though, have a ray that moves to the southwest. Once he discovered this, he began measuring the direction and length of fundamental rays around a huge assortment of items. He discovered that the fundamental ray of iron went to magnetic south, indicating that the rays were caused by the earth's magnetism.

You can test this for yourself by asking a friend to place a silver or copper coin under a cloth. Hold your pendulum over the cloth and slowly move the pendulum around the hidden coin. If you can sense the fundamental ray, the pendulum will start moving as soon as the pendulum is over it. If the pendulum moves from side to side on an east-west axis, the coin will be a silver one. If it moves from southwest to northeast, the coin will be copper. I find this experiment difficult, but have several friends who succeed more often than chance would tend to indicate.

Abbé Mermet regarded the fundamental ray as being his greatest discovery. Close behind this was what he called the "mental ray." The mental ray is a ray that moves from the object to the brain of the dowser. Mermet was not able to determine if the ray went from the brain to the object, or the other way

Figure 13A: Dowsing with the Various Rays

around. It was Mermet's belief that we are all inter-connected by these invisible rays of energy. This could provide an explanation of telepathy, with the thoughts traveling from one person to another along the mental ray.

A colleague of Mermet's, Abbé Bouly, discovered another ray that he called the "luminous ray." This is an invisible ray that comes from the sun, or any other light source, to every other body.

The "witness ray" is a ray that links two objects of the same item. For instance, if you placed two quarters and two pennies on a table, a witness ray would link the two quarters to each other, and another witness ray would link the two pennies. This is why many dowsers like to carry a "witness" with them. If they are looking for gold, for example, they would hold an item made of gold in one hand to help them locate it in the field.

Abbé Mermet also mentions a "vertical column" that is found above and below every object. When this column is not present, it is a sign of a magnetic disturbance which can influence the pendulum and adversely affect the results.

SERIAL NUMBERS AND ROTATION

Many dowsers believe that every object has its own special serial number that can be determined by the pendulum. For instance, Abbé Mermet claimed that silver has a serial number of six.[1] He found that if you hold your pendulum over an item made of silver, it will oscillate six times, pause for a moment, and then gyrate six times. It will then pause and start the cycle again and continue doing this for as long as you are prepared to hold your pendulum over it. You will get better results at determining serial numbers if you use a pendulum with a cord no longer than seven inches.

The first movements are the important ones, as the direction of the rotations can change when the experiment is continued. In the above example, if the silver is pure, the first gyrations will be in a clock-wise direction. If the silver is impure, the first gyrations will be in a counter-clockwise direction. If you are left-handed, pure silver will cause counter-clock-wise gyrations, and impure silver clockwise.

Abbé Mermet was the first to write about the phenomenon of series, but it is believed to have been independently discovered by several researchers in France and Germany in the nineteenth century.[2]

The problem with the serial numbers is that they vary from person to person. We have already discovered how we can influence the pendulum with our minds. If we believe that items of silver cause the pendulum to create a series of six, we can unconsciously make that happen. Another problem is that different objects can have the same serial number. T. C. Lethbridge amusingly recounts one occasion when his pendulum gave the serial number of eleven, the number of gold. When he dug in the spot suggested by the pendulum, he found a female beetle, which also has a serial number of eleven.[3]

Bruce Copen also comments on another problem in his book *The Practical Pendulum*. He says that if the dowser stands in the path of the object's fundamental ray, the serial number will increase by some twenty-five percent.[4]

Serial numbers are further complicated by the fact that different dowsers have their own methods of determining them. Pierre Beasse, a famous French dowser, placed his left forefinger on the object being analyzed and this caused his pendulum to swing. He would then raise his finger and place it down again, causing the pendulum to gyrate. Using his method, he decided that silver had a serial number of three.

Imagine the problems in analyzing compound objects when the experts cannot agree on something as simple as silver.

It is no wonder that people have become confused and frustrated with rays and serial numbers, particularly when they felt they could dowse but failed to detect the rays, or attempted to work out serial numbers and found their numbers were quite different from those of the author of the book they were studying. Their frustration is not surprising when even the authorities cannot agree.

Experiment with the rays and with the serial numbers. If you find you can make use of them, prepare a chart of common substances with their serial numbers which you can use for reference. However, if you can't make any use of the serial numbers, simply ignore them completely. It will make no difference to your ultimate success as a dowser.

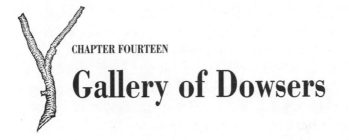

CHAPTER FOURTEEN

Gallery of Dowsers

I have many friends who are dowsers, which makes it difficult to choose just a few to mention here. I have included the following three, partly because of their ability and professionalism, but also because they demonstrate three different types of dowsing. Albino Gola is a professional dowser who specializes in detecting earth radiations. Docc Hilford is a busy man who dowses for relaxation after a hectic work schedule. He specializes in dowsing for historical artifacts. Brian Reid is a professional dowser who specializes in locating water and oil. All three are able to dowse for many other things, but have special areas of expertise.

ALBINO GOLA

Dowsers are able to work in many different fields. Albino Gola is a good example of this. He is a building biologist, Electro-Biology Environmental Inspector, and dowsing consultant. He is a Life Member and Past President of the New Zealand Society of Dowsing and Radionics, Inc. Albino's specialty is radiations from the earth.

He became interested in the field originally because of his own health problems. A friend suggested that he contact a color healer. Rather skeptically he sent a sample of his handwriting and a small piece of hair to the healer who lived 150 miles away. Two weeks later his good health returned. Albino found it hard to believe that someone who lived so far away could cure him. He visited the color healer and began to study different methods of healing. He very quickly discovered radiesthesia.

Thirty years ago, he joined a dowsing society and attended their classes. He found it difficult in the beginning. He could use a pendulum, but could not make a dowsing rod work. For a month he tried desperately hard with no success. As soon as he decided to give up, the rod started working for him. It took him a long time to understand this occurrence. Originally, he was willing the rod to work with sheer determination. As soon as he relaxed and allowed it to work, it did.

Shortly after this someone suggested that he dowse his own house as his family was always getting colds in winter. This acquaintance talked about "underwater streams." Albino's first question was, "What's that?" He tested the house and discovered there was a stream. Even worse, the stream forked under the house, compounding the problems. He made his first coil, which helped a little. Coils are designed to balance the energy from the cosmic principle. He kept on experimenting and improving his

ALBINO GOLA MAP DOWSES.

coils. Gradually, this became his main interest.

He carried on studying and now spends a great deal of his time teaching others with courses and lectures.

It sometimes hurts, but nowadays he is used to the skepticism of others. Albino says, "Usually, the people who don't believe me are the same people who eventually support me."

Recently, a couple visited him because of the wife's ill-health. The husband paced up and down, openly hostile. When Albino said there was radioactivity in a corner of their living room, the man told Albino that he was a charlatan. Albino continued, telling the couple what they should do to protect the house from harmful radiation. He made them an environmental stress harmonizer, which is a sophisticated coil, and told them to check the corner of the living room when they got back home.

The following morning the wife phoned Albino. She said her husband had never apologized to anyone in his entire life, and was not about to start. However, as soon as they returned home the previous day, the man had gone straight to the back of the garage, and removed a large box. Inside the box was a faulty fire alarm that had been emitting radioactivity. It was this radioactivity that Albino was picking up in the living room, which was on the other side of the wall.

The couple had not known how to dispose of the defective fire alarm, as the company they bought it from was no longer in business. Eventually, they wrapped it in newspaper, put it in a box in the garage and forgot all about it.

Albino has a store of similar stories, which he tells with understandable pride. He enjoys helping other people. In fact, for many years he worked semi-professionally on a goodwill offering basis and many times received five or ten dollars for a device that cost him thirty or forty to make. He is very happy that for the last three years he has been able to work full-time in a field that he loves.

He is now working internationally from his office in Auckland, New Zealand. With map dowsing he can help people anywhere in the world.

Recently, a client, who represented a company that was planning to develop a large piece of land in Australia, came to him for advice. They had spent fifteen thousand dollars drilling a well that failed to produce any water. Albino was able to tell them not only where to find water, but also advised them that a large piece of the land contained harmful radiations. Confirmation of this came when a Geiger counter detected a very high reading in the area Albino had indicated. The company moved to another area, that Albino, and a variety of electronic instruments, showed to be safe.

Albino manufactures two types of environmental stress harmonizers. One is very small, about the size of a fountain pen, and people carry these with them to counteract radiation and achieve a feeling of wellness. People who use them report that they have more energy and think more clearly. Albino made the first of these for a woman who suffered from air sickness and had to travel frequently on business. This first one did not help very much, but he developed a more advanced model that completely solved the problem.

In fact, when the woman had her purse stolen in London, she was more concerned about getting a replacement harmonizer than she was with her lost traveler's checks, credit cards, and passport.

Albino does not mass-produce these personal stress harmonizers, as each one needs to be tuned to the individual. If he cannot tune it correctly to the person, he refuses to sell it.

Albino has a great sense of integrity. He believes that when you dowse for yourself, you are responsible for your own actions. When you dowse for someone else, you are still just as responsible for your actions. He finds that almost ninety-nine percent of his students drop out because they are afraid of accepting responsibility. He also finds that the ego is the enemy of most dowsers. As soon as they think they know everything, they start making mistakes.

When Albino dowses, his aim is always to find the underlying cause, rather than simply treat the symptoms. He says that ill health is always a combination of many things. Usually, though, one or two factors come in very strongly. Mental stress is a major factor, plus lei line radiation from underground streams, and geopathic stress, which is a distortion from natural earth radiations. When people stay in these areas for a long time, their health starts to suffer. Some people are very sensitive and get affected very quickly. Other people take a great deal of time. Albino is delighted that scientific devices are now confirming the radiation that dowsers are able to pick up. Scientists are also well aware of the harmful effects of earth radiations.

Albino's larger environmental stress harmonizer is attached to the house it is designed to protect. It also harmonizes the immune systems of the people who live in the house. The occupants have to touch the coil for a few minutes every day. The people with these stress harmonizers are not only protected from harmful radiations, but are also more tranquil and calm. This is because the coil seems to harmonize the entire house.

Albino jokingly refers to his stress harmonizers as "coincidence coils." When people put them in their homes, they notice a difference, but generally say that it is simply a coincidence. Even when the health of someone with a life-threatening illness improves, some people still call it a coincidence.

Albino's favorite dowsing instrument is the V-shaped rod. He says this completes a full circle with both hands holding the rod. The pendulum is held by just one hand, of course. Albino says this allows other energies to affect the dowser, and other people are able to influence the movements. He demonstrates this effectively in his workshops. If he asks each person individually to test an apple and assess its quality, everyone gives a different answer. However, if Albino tests the apple and asks everybody to dowse his question, they all produce the same result.

He relates this to people listening to different stations on the radio. When he announces his result, suddenly everyone is on the same frequency and receives the same answer. This is why Albino prefers the rod. By using both hands, there is no interference. He has complete control between his higher mind and the subject he is dowsing. In other words, his mental radio is tuned to the right frequency.

Albino also uses the analogy of radio stations when discussing serial numbers. Each of us is tuned to a different frequency, and consequently, when we test for serial numbers, we must get different answers. Our answers will be correct for us, but not necessarily for anyone else. The fact that we are all on different frequencies also explains why some peoples' rods go upwards as a dowsing response, while other people experience a downward pull. Consequently, as dowsers, we all need to find out for ourselves what the right response is for us.

In the last four or five years, Albino has discovered a ray of harmful radiation that is man-made. Because of the huge amount of technology available today, Albino has found this ray in many homes. It causes depression and many other problems in the people who live in the path of these lines. He calls it an electromagnetic ray. It passes from one large electrical source, such as a transformer, to another.

Albino had a remarkable experience with someone who lived in the path of one of these electro-magnetic fields. A teacher came to see him as a last resort. His doctor had given him three to six weeks to live, as chemotherapy and cobalt treatment had ceased to work on his brain tumor.

The patient was so weak that his brother had to help him into Albino's office. On the house plan that he brought with him, Albino found underground water radiations, and also felt that the man was affected by a field coming between two transformers. The patient denied it, saying that he had lived in the house for eleven years and would certainly know if they were there. Albino suggested he check. The following day the man phoned him and said that he had sighted a power station out of sight, on top of a hill in one direction. When he looked in the opposite direction, he could see a transformer between two pylons half a mile away. When the patient compared it to the yellow line Albino had drawn on his plan, he discovered it matched exactly.

Albino made him an environmental stress harmonizer. Ten days later, Albino called him to see how he was. The man's wife told him that he and his daughter were riding bicycles to the hospital for a test. Less than two weeks earlier, this same man had to be partially carried into Albino's office. Three months later the doctors cleared him. He is still alive and well today and is back working as a teacher. He still has a yearly checkup.

Albino has developed a system to test himself before dowsing. Before starting, he asks: "Am I positive or am I negative?" "Is harmful radiation affecting me?" "Am I allowed to dowse?" "Should I dowse?" He calls these questions his safety valve. Albino dowses only when he receives the correct response to these questions. He knows from experience that if he is feeling unwell or is worried, he will not receive the correct answers from his dowsing rod. Albino has taught these questions to many people in his lectures and workshops over the years and they are now being used internationally.

Albino has good advice for people who are just starting out in dowsing. He suggests they start by reading as much as they can on the subject. They should then contact a dowsing association and learn from their courses. If possible, they should also spend time with a professional dowser. They should not accept anything at face value, but should determine the truth for themselves. This is because what is right for one dowser is not necessarily correct for another. Albino believes that if they are serious and sincere and follow this procedure, they will achieve success.

He warns that it is hard work. At times it can be easy, but it can also be very frustrating and difficult. When dowsing you have to think, be very thorough, and ensure that your mental attitude and motives are right. You also have to be very certain when dealing with another person that you have permission to use this energy for the betterment of this person. You also need integrity. Albino says that a special moment comes when you can call yourself a dowser. This happens when you are prepared to put your findings on paper and place it in front of your client before saying anything.

Albino does this every day. Clients come to see him and give him a map of their property and their name. He map dowses the plan and writes down his findings before talking with them.

When Albino teaches his students how to use the pendulum, he shows them how to test for positive and negative responses over a battery and a magnet. He suspends his pendulum over the positive end of the battery without asking any questions and simply observes what reaction the pendulum gives. He then holds it over the positive pole of the magnet and sees if it gives the same response. If he gets the same response, he then asks the pendulum "Am I positive?" Finally, he asks it: "Is my name Albino Gola?"

Using this method gives Albino four ways to determine and confirm the "yes" movement of his pendulum. All four movements of the pendulum need to be identical for Albino to be satisfied that his pendulum is giving the correct "yes" response.

Something is wrong if someone receives, for instance, a clockwise gyration over the positive end of a battery, but then receives the same movement over the negative end. This problem could be caused by negative thinking, ill health, or harmful radiation.

Albino calls dowsing a "micro science," as it is able to pick up minute traces of radiation that modern technology is only now able to measure. However, dowsers have been able to pick it up for many years.

Albino Gola is a happy man because he is doing what he loves. His work with both individuals and corporations is steadily increasing as his reputation expands. With the rapid increase in technology, he is certain that he will be kept busy for as long as he wants to be.

DOCC HILFORD

Docc is a large man, about six foot four in height, with a good, strong physique. It is easy to imagine him as a keen football player in his college days. His large collection of dowsing instruments attests to his physical stamina and strength. One of his Y-shaped rods is almost five feet long! However, he is equally at home with a small, delicate-looking silver pendulum that he made himself.

DOCC HILFORD USES A PENDULUM AND DOWSING ROD IN THE DESERT.

He lives in Phoenix, Arizona, and whenever his many business interests allow, he goes out into the desert dowsing for Native American artifacts, such as arrowheads and pottery shards.

Docc began to dowse after watching a professional water diviner and driller in action in Utah. This man thoroughly enjoyed teaching Docc the basics, as no one had ever asked him to be taught how to dowse before.

Docc is a busy man, making his living as an entertainer, public speaker, and publisher of *The New Invocation* magazine. He also promotes a large annual convention in Scottsdale that attracts registrants from all around the world. His entrepreneurial skills take him all over the United States, and he always travels with at least one pendulum.

With this, he is able to determine in advance the outcome of important business meetings, decide which bookings to accept, and what foods he should eat to keep fit and healthy while on the road.

Docc can never be serious for long and often entertains people with his pendulum. I once saw him locating quarters that had been placed under a rug in a hotel lobby. Five quarters had been hidden, but to everyone's amazement Docc successfully found seven!

Docc, with his enthusiasm and zest for life, has introduced many people to dowsing. Many of the hard-nosed business people he deals with on a daily basis are extremely skeptical until Docc produces his pendulum and demonstrates his ability. After amazing the skeptics, Docc is happy to show them how to dowse. He attributes some of his success to the fact that everyone remembers him, and this is partly due to his skill as a dowser.

Docc also uses dowsing as a way of relaxing. "Time stands still for me when I'm out in the desert," he explains. "The more relaxed and at peace I am, the more successful I am at dowsing."

Docc uses dowsing in every area of his life. "It enables me to get in touch with my inner being," he explains. "If I am not sure what decision to make, I'll ask my pendulum. It may not give me the answer I want, but it will tell me which decision is best for everyone concerned. If I follow its advice, I can't go wrong."

BRIAN REID

My friend Brian Reid lives in a small farming town. He is known to everyone there and letters addressed to "Water Diviner" always reach him. He cannot remember a time when he did not dowse, as his father was a keen dowser before him. (Incidentally, some of Brian's children and grandchildren also dowse, making him part of a four-generation family of dowsers.) Brian began at the age of five using a V-shaped rod cut from an apple tree in the back yard. His father used to do his dowsing at night, because members of the local church considered it to be the work of the devil.

Brian is now seventy years old, but is as busy as ever. In the last twelve months, he has located the sites of eleven hundred wells, mainly water for farms. He also dowses for oil and has done valuable work for the Astral Oil Company. The dowsing he has done for them has included map-dowsing from photographs of the area, airplane dowsing from 35,000 feet, and dowsing on their exploration sites.

In his spare time, he dowses to locate forgotten grave sites, which he restores. He does this as a voluntary service to the community. Brian has completed an entire cemetery of early pioneers in this way. The records had been lost and Brian realigned the long forgotten graves with his angle rods. However, most of this work is in locating the grave sites of pioneers who died a hundred or more years ago and were buried somewhere on the family farm.

Brian does not have a favorite dowsing tool. He uses whatever best suits his purpose for the job at hand. He uses brass angle rods for most of his field work, and also has a three-foot-long brass bobbing stick for determining locations and depth.

His bobbing stick will indicate directions for him from as far as one thousand yards away. He calls the bobbing stick his "cross-examiner" as it is so revealing for him. With it he can locate sites of primary water,[1] burial sites, oil, or anything else he is searching for.

Brian frequently uses his angle rods, V-shaped rod, bobbing stick, and pendulum to confirm his findings. If he locates a site with his angle rods, he will then check the site again with his pendulum and bobbing stick to see if he gets the same response. He explains that drilling is very expensive, and he likes to be one hundred percent certain before telling someone to spend money on drilling a well. He does not hand dowse. Brian particularly enjoys map dowsing because, as he says, "it is so precise."

His dowsing sessions usually begin with map dowsing. Then he visits the site, dowsing in the car on the way. A single angle rod tells him when to stop. Then he will use his bobbing stick to tell him how far away the water is, and if it is primary or ground water. His bobbing stick will also tell him where to find the best source of water on the property. Most of his wells produce from 1,000 to 6,000 gallons an hour. This is an excellent supply, as a three-hundred-cow farm can get by with just three hundred gallons of water per hour. Once his bobbing stick has provided this information, it is a simple matter to locate and mark the correct spot to drill.

He usually uses a single angle rod when map dowsing. He does not use a pointer. Instead, he uses the tip of the downward branch of the rod as a locator. This is held about half an inch from the surface of the map. With this he has located oil and vast reservoirs of primary water around the world. Unfortunately, many of his findings have been discounted by local politicians who have a vested interest in maintaining existing sources of water, which often needs expensive treatment, rather than drilling for primary water, which is pure. This small-mindedness annoys him, but he accepts it the same way he has accepted the skepticism of others throughout his life.

Brian is able to laugh at skeptics as his sites produce. Recently, he visited three holes that had been drilled, on the advice of geologists at the cost of many thousands of dollars. None of them produced anything.

His grandchildren enjoy playing a special game with him. When they come to visit, they take a single petal from a flower in their beautiful, well-kept flower garden and put it down the back of his neck without letting him see it. Brian then takes a single angle rod and walks around his garden, quickly finding the flower the petal was taken from. It is an impressive test, and one his little friends never tire of seeing.

Another test he often does involves a hot water bottle. This is filled with either hot or cold water. The top is not screwed in tightly, allowing a little bit to dribble out. (This is because it is almost impossible to dowse still water.) Brian dowses over these with his angle rods. If the water is cold, the angle rod in his left hand will turn ninety degrees. If the water is hot, his right hand angle rod will do the same.

He has successfully performed this feat for scientists, who then asked him to find a dog bone buried

BRIAN REID USES RODS AND A WITNESS STONE.

in one of several piles of sawdust. This was an easy test for Brian to accomplish, as he simply asked his rods to find calcium. Brian does not mind being tested in this way but regards it as playing, rather than serious dowsing.

Brian's main interest these days is in locating primary water, which he says can be found all over the world, even in desert areas. He believes that vast areas of the world will become fertile when people start making use of this incredibly pure water. As it is so readily available everywhere, long, expensive pipelines are not necessary because the water travels through its own, natural arterial system.

He does not know where this water comes from originally, believing that it may have come about as a residue from volcanoes under the earth's surface. These eruptions create gases which either escape to the surface as gas or turn into primary water. Brian thinks that perhaps these gases are electrically and chemically fired into the rock itself and the rock fuses the water out. He uses coal mines as an example, where rock has been found that is like a sponge full of water. This is a hypothesis at present, but Brian is convinced it is the answer.

It took him almost two years to be able to dowse for primary water with the accuracy he required. It was his driller who first noticed that Brian's angle rods vibrated over each other whenever he located primary water fissures. With ordinary running water, his angle rods simply cross each other in the usual manner.

THESE ARE USED AS WITNESS STONES BY BRIAN REID.

Brian is famed for his accuracy and, strangely, this has caused him to be attacked from an unexpected quarter. Many welldrillers prefer to drill deeper than necessary, because of the extra money they make. When Brian says that water will be found at sixty three feet, for instance, the person who is paying for the job knows that water will be found at that depth. Brian expects his driller to drill to approximately that depth and then test with a compressor. Usually, Brian's depth will be exact, and only occasionally will the driller have to drill just a little bit more. Consequently, the well-driller cannot stop at the first appearance of water, or alternatively drill too deep. Brian insists that they drill to exactly the depth he states. Nowadays, Brian uses his own driller whenever he can. Because his work takes him around the country a great deal, this is not always possible.

Brian is not particularly interested in the reasons why dowsing works. He simply does it. He believes it is caused partly by the influence of the poles, creating a magnetic influence, but holds no strong views on the subject. The reactions he gets from his dowsing instruments are the most extreme I have ever witnessed. On more than one occasion the tip of a crystal pendulum has been blown off as part of his dowsing response.

Recently, I saw him dowsing with a V-shaped rod that twisted about itself three times in his hands when he was over an oil find. It would have twisted even farther, but the reaction was so strong he was forced to let go. I have the dowsing rod as a souvenir of this unforgettable occasion.

This occurred when Brian was dowsing for oil close to his home. He began by map-dowsing with a single angle rod. As the site was on farm land only a few miles away, we decided to visit it and confirm what the angle rod said. Brian began by locating a circle approximately 120 feet in diameter. He went around this circle with his angle rods and found two fissures containing oil. Again using his rods, he found the best place inside the circle to drill. It was over this spot that his V-shaped rod twisted three times. With his bobbing stick he determined that the oil was 2,400 feet underground. He then determined the type of rock that would have to be drilled through. He did this by holding up samples of different types of rock and asking an angle rod if this type of rock was present. These sample rocks act as witnesses for him. The entire exercise on site took only ten minutes.

Brian's neighbors have good reason to be thankful to him. On one occasion, when he was dowsing for oil

BRIAN REID'S
V-SHAPED
ROD TWISTS
IN HIS HANDS
DURING A
STRONG
DOWSING
RESPONSE.

over photographs taken from 35,000 feet in the air, he suddenly became aware of a good supply of primary water on a farm less than two miles from his home. He phoned the farmer and told him about it. Within minutes the farmer called on him to talk about it. A hole was drilled and the farmer is now enjoying a bountiful supply of pure water.

Usually, after a dowsing session, Brian provides his clients with a graph showing the formation of the ground under the surface. He uses an angle rod to determine the depth of the top soil, and all the other formations the driller will have to go through to reach water. The rod even tells him the quality of the different formations. For instance, if it is sandstone, the rod will tell him if it is good quality sandstone or "green" sandstone, which is too soft and creates problems for the driller.

In a long and varied career, Brian has been a butcher, spent time in the army, worked as a farmer, and then a bridge-builder for the railways. During his time with the railways, he dowsed for culverts and other buried items that his employers had forgotten about. His greatest happiness has come from dowsing, which is why he is still so busy, even though his health has slowed him down a bit and he tires more easily. Nowadays after a dowsing session, Brian frequently lies down and sleeps for a couple of hours. He has had serious health problems in the past, and says he wouldn't be alive today if it had not been for his strong interest in dowsing. He does not drink or smoke, but likens dowsing to these, saying that it is his "addiction."

Although he is now in his seventies, Brian's eyes still light up with enthusiasm whenever he talks about dowsing. The years fall away and he is like an eager teenager again. His enthusiasm for dowsing is as keen as ever, and he has a strong desire to introduce as many people as possible to dowsing. This year he is hoping to locate just two wells a day, but the demand for his services is so great that he is likely to be just as busy in the next twelve months as he ever has been.

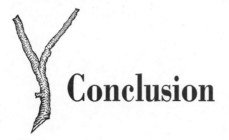

Conclusion

I hope that with the help of this book you have been able to enter the fascinating world of rhabdomancy—dowsing. It is an art that has helped mankind for thousands of years. You can use it to help others today. You can help others by dowsing for water, oil, gold, or other desired items. You can find lost articles, and dowse for health, wealth, and happiness.

Expect a certain amount of ridicule from others. Dowsers have experienced this throughout history. The best solution is to become a really good dowser. Read everything that is available, spend time watching and talking with other dowsers, and practice as much as you can. Join a dowsing society. As your skills develop remain modest and let your successes speak for themselves.

You are embarking on an interest that will enhance your life in many different ways. I wish you all the success in the world.

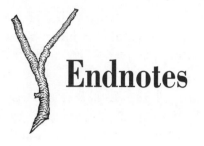

Endnotes

INTRODUCTION

1. In his book *Psychic Breakthroughs Today*, D. Scott Rogo described a research project where a woman who dowsed for winning horses was put to a test. Unbeknownst to her, the panel also enlisted the aid of two psychology students, one of whom was an expert at horse racing. Over a two-week period, the dowser and the two students tried to pick the winners of eighty races. The dowser was crestfallen, as she picked only four winners out of eight races on her best day. However, she did better than both of the students. The student who knew nothing about racing had a success rate of 17.5 percent. The racing buff managed 28.8 percent, and the crestfallen dowser achieved 40 percent! *Psychic Breakthroughs Today* was published by The Aquarian Press, Wellingborough, in 1987, pages 43–44.

2. Other references to rods in the Bible that possibly relate to dowsing are Exodus XVII: 1–6, Hosea IV:

12, Psalm CXXV: 3, Numbers XVII and Numbers XX: 1–12.

3. An English translation of *De Re Metallica* by Herbert Clark Hoover and Lou Henry Hoover was published by Dover Publications, New York, in 1950.

4. *Second Essay on Unsucceeding Experiments* by Robert Boyle. Quoted in *An Encyclopedia of Occultism,* by Lewis Spence, originally published in 1920 by George Routledge and Sons Limited, London. Reprinted 1960 by The Citadel Press, Secaucus, N.J., page 128.

5. Martine de Bertereau's discovery of the healing springs at Chateau Thierry was witnessed by many people, as she asked the leading citizens to verify her findings. One of these people, Claude Galien, a doctor, was so impressed with the discovery that he wrote a book about it called *La Découverte des Eaux Minérales de Chateau-Thierry et de Leurs Propriétés (The Discovery of the Mineral Waters of Chateau-Thierry and their Properties),* which was published in Paris in 1630.

6. *Dowsing: New Light on an Ancient Art,* by Tom Williamson, Robert Hale Limited, London, 1993, pages 32–35.

7. *The Divining Rod*, by Sir William Barrett and Theodore Besterman. Originally published in 1926. Reprinted, with a new introduction by Leslie Shepard, by University Books, Inc., New Hyde Park, N.Y., 1968, pages 27–29.

8. *Max Maven's Book of Fortunetelling,* by Max Maven, Prentice-Hall, New York, 1992, page 208.

9. *The Confessions of an English Opium-eater,* by Thomas de Quincey. Originally published in 1822. My edition was published by The Folio Society, London, 1948, page 63.

10. *Water in England,* by Dorothy Hartley, Macdonald and Jane's Publishers Limited, London. First published 1964. Revised edition 1978, pages 382–385.

11. *Encyclopedia of Psychic Science,* by Nandor Fodor, University Books, Inc., New York, 1966, page 99.

12. *The Divining Rod,* by Sir William Barrett and Theodore Besterman, page 203.

13. *The Divining Rod,* by Sir William Barrett and Theodore Besterman, pages 223–224.

14. *Letters on the Truth Contained in the Popular Superstitions,* by Professor Herbert Mayo, Cranbourne and Company, London, 1851.

15. *Water in England,* by Dorothy Hartley, page 385.

16. Roche-Zeitung, Hoffmann La Roche, Basle. *House Journal,* 1972–73 edition.

17. Roche-Zeitung. 1972–73 issue. A detailed account of this company's dowsing experiences can be found in *The Divining Hand,* by Christopher Bird, E. P. Dutton and Company, New York, 1979, pages 50–53.

18. *The Beginner's Handbook of Dowsing*, by Joseph Baum, Crown Publishers, Inc., New York, 1974, page 6.

19. *Dowsing,* by W. H. Trinder, British Society of Dowsers, London, 1955. Mr Trinder knew Miss Evelyn Penrose and relates how she told him that walking over an underground silver mine in Canada for the first time felt as if a "red-hot knife" had been plunged into her foot, pages 84–85. On page 98 of the same book is a letter from a government minister congratulating Miss Penrose on her talents at map divining.

20. *Arthur C. Clarke's World of Strange Powers*, by John Fairley and Simon Welfare, William Collins Sons and Company Limited, London, 1984, pages 178–181.

21. *Max Maven's Book of Fortunetelling*, by Max Maven, page 208.

22. *Comment Devenir Sourcier, Ce Quai J'ai Vu, Ce Que J'ai Fait (How to Become a Dowser–What I've Seen and What I've Done)*, by Armand Viré, Librairie J-B Baillière, Paris, 1948.

23. *ESP: Your Sixth Sense*, by Brad Steiger, Award Books, New York, 1966, pages 78–79.

24. Probably the best book on the subject from a skeptical point of view is *Water Witching U.S.A.*, by Evon Z. Vogt and Ray Hyman, University of Chicago Press, Chicago, 1959. Revised edition 1979. Interesting skeptical articles can be found in *E.S.P., Seers and Psychics*, by Milbourne

Christopher, Crowell and Company, New York, 1970, *Fads and Fallacies in the Name of Science*, by Martin Gardner, Dover Publications, New York, 1957, *Paranormal Borderlands of Science*, edited by Kendrick Frazier, Prometheus Books, Buffalo, New York, 1981, and *Secrets of the Supernatural*, by Joe Nickell with John F. Fischer, Prometheus Books, Buffalo, New York, 1988. An excellent skeptical article called "Dowsing: A Review of Experimental Research," by George P. Hansen, can be found in the *Journal of the Society for Psychical Research*, 51, pages 343–367, 1982.

CHAPTER ONE

1. *The Elements of Dowsing,* by Le Vicomte Henry de France. Translated by A. H. Bell, G. Bell and Sons Limited, London, 1948, page 4.

2. *Aquavideo: Locating Underground Water,* by Verne Cameron, El Cariso Publications, Elsinore, 1970. This book, published posthumously, describes the aurameter in detail and also outlines some of the incredible successes the author had in dowsing for water in desert regions.

3. *The Divining Rod,* by Sir William Barrett and Theodore Besterman, page 153.

4. *Modern Dowsing,* by Raymond C. Willey, Esoteric Publications, Sedona, 1976, pages 53–54.

5. *Modern Dowsing,* by Raymond C. Willey, page 55.

6. *The Dowsing and Healing Manual,* by Alanna Moore, page 58.

Chapter Two

1. *Papers and Transactions of the International Folklore Congress.* International Folklore Society, London, 1892. Article by Marian Roalfe Cox, pages 439–442.

Chapter Three

1. *The Complete Book of Dowsing and Divining,* by Peter Underwood, Rider and Company, London, 1980, page 113.

2. *ESP: Your Sixth Sense,* by Brad Steiger, Award Books, New York, 1966, pages 77–78.

3. *Practical Dowsing: A Symposium,* edited by A. H. Bell, G. Bell and Sons Limited, London, 1965, page 56.

4. *Diviner on Brink of Priceless Find,* by Barry Leader. Article in *Farm Equipment News*, Auckland. Issue 326, October 1993.

5. *Practical Dowsing: A Symposium,* edited by A. H. Bell, page 44.

Chapter Four

1. *Principles and Practice of Radiesthesia,* by Abbé Mermet. Originally published in French in 1935. English translation by Mark Clement, first pub-

lished in 1959. My copy was published by Element Books, Longmead, Dorset in 1987, pages 136–137.

2. *Arthur C. Clarke's World of Strange Powers,* by John Fairley and Simon Welfare, page 181.

3. *Pendulum Power,* by Greg Nielsen and Joseph Polansky, Destiny Books, New York, 1977, pages 51–52. Verne Cameron was a well known Californian water diviner. His twenty-year battle to provide water for the empty Lake Elsinore is outlined in *The Divining Hand,* by Christopher Bird, E. P. Dutton, New York, 1979, pages 53–57.

4. *Pendulum Power,* by Greg Nielsen and Joseph Polansky, page 108.

5. *Practical Dowsing: A Symposium,* edited by A. H. Bell, pages 98–99.

6. *C. Clarke's World of Strange Powers,* by John Fairley and Simon Welfare, pages 181–182.

7. *Occult Illustrated Dictionary,* by Harvey Day, Kaye and Ward Limited, London, 1975, page 38.

8. *Diviner on Brink of Priceless Find,* by Barry Leader, Article in *Farm Equipment News*, Auckland. Issue 326, October 1993.

9. *Principles and Practice of Radiesthesia,* by Abbé Mermet, pages 207–208.

CHAPTER FIVE

1. The exact dates that Marcellinus was pope are not accurately known. However, his period as pope marked a brief tranquil stage in a violent era

where Christians were being attacked. It is believed that he was a victim of this persecution and became a martyr. His body was buried in the cemetery of St. Priscilla in Rome, and he is today regarded as a saint. His feast day is April 26th.

2. *The Divining Hand,* by Christopher Bird, page 123.

3. *Pendulum Power,* by Greg Nielsen and Joseph Polansky, page 25.

4. A number of interesting experiments are included in *How to Develop Your Psychic Power,* by Richard Webster, Martin Breese Limited, London, 1988 and *Pendulum Power for the Psychic Entertainer,* by Richard Webster, Brookfield Press, Auckland, 1990. A chapter of pendulum experiments is included in *How to Produce Miracles,* by Ormond McGill, A. S. Barnes and Company, New York, 1976.

5. T. C. Lethbridge (1901–1971) wrote several fascinating books on dowsing, archaeology and parapsychology that are well worth reading. They are all published by Routledge and Kegan Paul, London. His books are: *Gogmagog: The Buried Gods*, 1957, *Ghost and Ghoul,* 1961, *Witches: Investigating an Ancient Religion*, 1962, *Ghost and Divining Rod,* 1963, *ESP: Beyond Time and Distance,* 1965, *A Step in the Dark,* 1967, *The Monkey's Tale: A Study in Evolution and Parapsychology,* 1969, and *The Power of the Pendulum,* 1976. There is also *The Essential T. C. Lethbridge,* edited by Tom Graves and Janet Hoult, 1980.

6. *The Divining Rod* by T. Forder Plowman. This is an article in the *Proceedings of the Bath Natural History and Antiquarian Field Club*, Bath, 1889. Volume VI, pages 414–415.

7. *The Divining Hand,* by Christopher Bird, pages 118–119.

CHAPTER SIX

1. *Supernature,* by Lyall Watson, Hodder and Stoughton Limited, London, 1973, page 111.

2. *Modern Dowsing,* by Raymond C. Willey, Esoteric Publications, Cottonwood, AZ, 1975, page 56.

3. *Supernature,* by Lyall Watson, page 118. *The Complete Book of Dowsing and Divining,* by Peter Underwood, page 86.

4. I learned this method from *Dowsing: One Man's Way,* by J. Scott Elliot, Neville Spearman, Jersey Limited, Jersey, 1977, pages 46–47. I find this method very practical and, when I do it, my hands do not quite touch. However, a friend of mine who learned this method from me finds that his hands do touch and, in fact, become locked together until he moves away from the site.

5. *Modern Dowsing,* by Raymond C. Willey, pages 52–54.

6. *The Complete Book of Dowsing and Divining,* by Peter Underwood, page 179.

7. *Encyclopedia of Psychic Science,* by Nandor Fodor, University Books, Inc., New York, 1966, page 98.

In 1930, Abbé Alexis Bouly founded the *Association des Amis de la Radiesthesie*, the first dowsing society in France. Three years later he was instrumental in forming the British Society of Dowsers. In 1950, at the age of 85, he was awarded a *Chevalier de La Legion d'Honneur* as a tribute to his work. This is France's highest honor.

8. *The Divining Hand,* by Christopher Bird, pages 109–110.

CHAPTER SEVEN

1. *The Beginner's Handbook of Dowsing,* by Joseph Baum, Crown Publishers, Inc., New York, 1974, page 6.

2. *The Dowsing and Healing Manual,* by Alanna Moore, Katoomba, Australia, 1987, page 7.

3. *Beyond the Occult,* by Colin Wilson, Bantam Press, division of Transworld Publishers Limited, London, 1988, pages 116–117.

4. *Beyond the Occult,* by Colin Wilson, page 117.

5. Ibid.

6. *Beyond Supernature,* by Lyall Watson, Hodder and Stoughton, London, 1986, pages 248–249.

7. *Modern Dowsing,* by Raymond C. Willey, page 192.

8. *The Beginner's Handbook of Dowsing,* by Joseph Baum, page 6.

CHAPTER NINE

1. *Water Divining and Other Dowsing,* by Ralph Whitlock, David and Charles Publishers Limited, Newton Abbott, 1982, page 51. Information about the sacred trees of the druids can be found in *Omens, Oghams and Oracles,* by Richard Webster, Llewellyn Publications, St. Paul, 1995.

2. *The Complete Book of Dowsing and Divining,* by Peter Underwood, Rider and Company, London, 1980, pages 95–96.

CHAPTER TEN

1. *The Secret of Life*, by Georges Lakhovsky, William Heinemann Limited, London, 1939, pages 5–13. Lakhovsky was a Russian born engineer who spent much of his life in Paris. His book came out just before the Second World War and, consequently, did not receive the recognition it deserved. Lakhovsky founded the science of radio-biology. In 1923, his first major invention, the radio-cellulo-oscillator, was demonstrated to cure geraniums that had been innoculated with cancer. The Lakhovsky loop used an oscillating circuit that created resonance and increased immunity and resistance to disease. Lakhovsky died in New York in 1942.

2. *The Practical Pendulum* by Dr. Bruce Copen, Academic Publications, Sussex, 1974, page 78. Dr. Copen has written a number of other books on

radiesthesia and earth radiations, including *Harmful Radiations and Their Elimination,* Academic Publications, 1962.

3. *Practical Dowsing: A Symposium,* edited by A. H. Bell. This book contains an article called "The Neutralisation of Harmful Rays" by A. D. Manning, which explains how to make copper coils.

4. *Dowsing: New Light on an Ancient Art,* by Tom Williamson, Robert Hale Limited, London, 1993, pages 50–51.

5. *Dowsing: New Light on an Ancient Art,* by Tom Williamson, page 56.

6. *Water Divining and Other Dowsing,* by Ralph Whitlock, page 39. W. H. Trinder says in his book *Dowsing,* published by the British Society of Dowsers, London, 1955, pages 81–82, that the rock is not radioactive and consequently, the explanation is not known.

7. *Introduction to Earth Rays,* by Rolf Gordon, Dulwich Health Society, London, n.d., page 16.

8. *Handbook of Psi Discoveries,* by Sheila Ostrander and Lynn Schroeder, Sphere Books Limited, London, 1974, page 210.

9. *How Cats Take to Water,* by Ralph Whitlock. This is an article from his syndicated column "Leisure," which appears in many newspapers. I found it in the *Guardian Weekly*, Auckland, August 1993.

10. *The Psychic Explorer,* by Jonathan Cainer and Carl Rider, Judy Piatkus Publishers Limited, London, 1988, page 128.

11. *Water Divining and other Dowsing,* by Ralph Whitlock, page 125.

12. *Principles and Practices of Radiesthesia,* by Abbé Mermet, page 167.

13. *Dowsing: One Man's Way,* by J. Scott Elliot, page 155.

14. *Dowsing,* by W.H. Trinder, pages 75–76.

15. *The Anatomy Coloring Book,* by W. Kapit and L. Elson, Harper and Row, New York, 1977. Other good books on anatomy include: *The Human Body,* by Isaac Asimov, New American Library, New York, *Esoteric Anatomy,* by Dr. Douglas Baker, Douglas Baker, Essendon, England, *Introduction to Human Anatomy,* by James Crouch, Mayfield Publishing Company, Palo Alto, Calif., *Anatomy and Physiology for Nurses,* by Evelyn Pearce, Faber and Faber, London, and the classic *Gray's Anatomy,* by Henry Gray, various publishers.

16. "Diagnostic Analysis with a Pendulum" is included as a chapter in *How to Use the Pendulum,* by Stella Askew, Health Reasearch, Mokelumne Hill, 1955, pages 29–30.

17. *Toward Balance,* by Rita J. McNamara, Samuel Weiser, Inc., York Beach, Maine, 1989, pages 17–69.

18. *Healing Words,* by Larry Dossey, M.D., Harper-San Francisco, San Francisco, 1994, pages XVII–XVIII, and 211–235.

Chapter Eleven

1. *The Divining Hand,* by Christopher Bird, pages 240–242.

2. *Dowsing: One Man's Way,* by J. Scott Elliot, Neville Spearman Jersey Limited, Jersey, 1977, pages 146–148.

3. *The Power of the Pendulum,* by T. C. Lethbridge, Routledge and Kegan Paul, New York, 1976. My edition is published by Arkana Books, London, 1984, page 24.

4. *Encyclopedia of Psychic Science,* by Nandor Fodor, page 99.

5. *Beyond Supernature,* by Lyall Watson, page 250.

6. *The Divining Hand,* by Christopher Bird, pages 240–242.

7. *Dowsing: New Light on an Ancient Art,* by Tom Williamson, Robert Hale Limited, London, 1993, pages 67–69.

8. *Dowsing and Church Archaeology,* by R. N. Bailey, E. Cambridge and H. D. Briggs Intercept, Dorset, 1988. A skeptical analysis of Denis Briggs' work can be found in *Forbidden Knowledge,* by Bob Couttie, Lutterworth Press, Cambridge, England, 1988, pages 87–88.

9. *Dowsing: New Light on an Ancient Art,* by Tom Williamson, Robert Hale Limited, London, 1993, pages 67–69.

10. *The Pattern of the Past*, by Guy Underwood, Sphere Books Limited, London, 1969. Abelard-

Schuman, New York, 1973. This landmark book
was the first written by a dowser explaining
exactly what he found at sacred sites. His study
of earth energies has been widely praised, but so
far few people have felt the desire to carry on
with his research. Maybe you will feel drawn to
explore this subject further.

11. "Dowsing the Way," by Sig Lonegren. An article
in *The World Atlas of Divination*, edited by John
Matthew's Headline Book Publishing PLC, London, 1992, page 207.

CHAPTER TWELVE

1. *Dowsing for Everyone,* by Harvey Howells, The
Stephen Greene Press, Brattleboro, Vermont,
1979, page 42.

2. *The Essential T. C. Lethbridge,* edited by Tom
Graves and Janet Hoult, Routledge and Kegan
Paul Limited, London, 1980, pages 124–125. *The
Power of the Pendulum,* by T. C. Lethbridge,
Arkana Books edition, pages 61–62.

3. *The Divining Hand,* by Christopher Bird, pages
141–143, Professor Tromp's book, *Psychical
Physics: A Scientific Analysis of Dowsing, Radiesthesia and Kindred Divining Phenomena,* was
published by Elsevier Publishing Company, New
York in 1949.

4. *The Divining Hand,* by Christopher Bird, page
238.

5. *How to Develop Your Psychic Power,* by Richard Webster, Martin Breese Limited, London, 1988, pages 40–44.

Chapter Thirteen

1. *Principles and Practice of Radiesthesia,* by Abbé Mermet, page 53.

2. *The Practical Pendulum,* by Dr. Bruce Copen, page 54. Le Vicomte Henry de France in *The Modern Dowser,* G. Bell and Sons Limited, London, 1930, also claims that the idea of a series is a very old one. Incidentally, for him, the series number of silver was seven.

3. *ESP: Beyond Time and Distance,* by T. C. Lethbridge 1965. This story is also recounted in *Water Divining and other Dowsing,* by Ralph Whitlock, page 42.

4. *The Practical Pendulum,* by Dr. Bruce Copen, page 55.

Chapter Fourteen

1. Primary water is water that is somehow formed inside rock strata. It was first investigated by Adolf Nordenskiöld, the nineteenth century explorer who was the first man to sail from Norway to the Pacific through the Northeast Passage. As well as being a famous arctic explorer he was also a geologist, geographer and professor of mineralogy at the Swedish State Museum. He wrote

an essay on the subject of primary water which caused him to be nominated for the Nobel Prize in physics.

Nordenskiöld was inspired by his father who was in charge of mining in Finland. He told his son that fresh water could always be found on the floors of some iron mines, even when they were below sea level when salt water would be expected.

In the twentieth century, the leading exponent of primary water is Stephan Riess who successfully located hundreds of sources of primary water in California, Nevada, and Arizona as well as in Israel and Egypt. Riess' theory is that water is being continually manufactured in rock strata when the right combination of temperature and pressure is present. This water is then forced into fissures in the rock where it can travel hundreds of miles. As this is moving water, it can be located by dowsers. A fascinating account of Stephan Riess' career can be found in *The Divining Hand,* by Christopher Bird.

Suggested Reading

Baerlein, E., and A.L.G. Dower. *Healing with Radionics.* Thorsons Publishers Limited, Wellingborough, 1980.

Bird, Christopher. *The Divining Hand.* E. P. Dutton, New York, 1979.

Barrett, Sir William and Besterman, Theodore. *The Divining Rod.* University Books, New Hyde Park, New York, 1968

Davies, Rodney. *Dowsing.* The Aquarian Press, London, 1991.

Elliot, J. Scott. *Dowsing One Man's Way.* Neville Spearman (Jersey) Limited, Jersey, 1977.

de France, Le Vicomte Henry. *The Elements of Dowsing.* G. Bell and Sons, London, 1948.

Graves, Tom. *Dowsing Techniques and Applications.* Turnstone Books, London, 1976.

Graves, Tom. *The Dowser's Workbook.* The Aquarian Press, London, 1989. Reprinted as *Discover Dowsing,* 1993.

Howells, Harvey. *Dowsing for Everyone.* The Stephen Greene Press. Brattleboro, Vermont, 1979.

Lethbridge, T.C. *The Power of the Pendulum.* Routledge and Kegan Paul, New York, 1976.

Nielsen, Greg and Joseph Polansky. *Pendulum Power.* Greg Nielsen and Destiny Books, New York, 1977.

Roberts, Kenneth. *Henry Gross and his Dowsing Rod.* Doubleday and Company, Inc., Garden City, New York, 1951.

Trinder, W.H. *Dowsing.* British Society of Dowsers, London, 1955.

Willey, Raymond C. *Modern Dowsing.* Esoteric Publications, Sedona, Arizona, 1976.

Williamson, Tom. *Dowsing: New Light on an Ancient Art.* Robert Hale Limited, London, 1993.

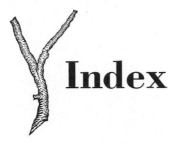

Index

195

Aura Reading for Beginners

Develop Your Psychic Awareness for Health & Success

Richard Webster

When you lose your temper, don't be surprised if a dirty red haze suddenly appears around you. If you do something magnanimous, your aura will expand. Now you can learn to see the energy that emanates off yourself and other people through the proven methods taught by Richard Webster in his psychic training classes.

Learn to feel the aura, see the colors in it, and interpret what those colors mean. Explore the chakra system, and how to restore balance to chakras that are over- or under-stimulated. Then you can begin to imprint your desires into your aura to attract what you want in your life.

1-56718-798-6
208 pp., 5³⁄₁₆ x 8, illus., appendix, bibliog., index $11.95

To order, call 1-877-NEW-WRLD

Prices subject to change without notice

Palm Reading for Beginners

Find the Future in the Palm of Your Hand

Richard Webster

Announce in any gathering that you read palms and you will be flocked by people thrilled to show you their hands. When you are have finished *Palm Reading for Beginners*, you will be able to look at anyone's palm (including your own) and confidently and effectively tell them about their personality, love life, hidden talents, career options, prosperity, and health.

Palmistry is possibly the oldest of the occult sciences, with basic principles that have not changed in 2,600 years. This step-by-step guide clearly explains the basics, as well as advanced research conducted in the past few years on such subjects as dermatoglyphics.

1-56718-791-9
264 pp., 5³⁄₁₆ x 8, softcover $13.95

Write Your Magic

The Hidden Power in Your Words

Richard Webster

Write your innermost dreams and watch them come true!
This book will show you how to use the incredible power of words to create the life that you have always dreamed about. We all have desires, hopes and wishes. Sadly, many people think theirs are unrealistic or unattainable. *Write Your Own Magic* shows you how to harness these thoughts by putting them to paper.

Once a dream is captured in writing it becomes a goal, and your subconscious mind will find ways to make it happen. From getting a date for Saturday night to discovering your purpose in life, you can achieve your goals, both small and large. You will also learn how to speed up the entire process by making a ceremony out of telling the universe what it is you want. With the simple instructions in this book, you can send your energies out into the world and magnetize all that is happiness, success, and fulfillment to you.

- Send your energies out into the universe with rituals, ceremonies, and spells
- Magnetize yourself so that your desires are attracted to you, while the things you do not want are repelled
- Create suitable spells for different purposes

0-7387-0001-0
5 ³⁄₁₆ x 8, 312 pp. $12.95

To order, call 1-877-NEW-WRLD

Pendulum Magic for Beginners

The Power to Achieve All Goals

Richard Webster

The pendulum is a simple, accurate, and versatile device consisting of a weight attached to a chain or thread. Arguably the most underrated item in the magician's arsenal, the pendulum can reveal information not found any other way. It can read energy patterns, extracting information from deep inside our subconscious.

This book will teach you how to perform apparent miracles such as finding lost objects, helping your potted plants grow better, protecting yourself from harmful foods, detecting dishonesty in others, and even choosing the right neighborhood. Explore past lives, recall dreams, release blocks to achieving happiness, and send your wishes out into the universe.

0-7387-0192-0
288 pp., 5 ³/₁₆ x 8, illus., index $13.95

To order, call 1-877-NEW-WRLD

Prices subject to change without notice

Is Your Pet Psychic?

Developing Psychic Communication with Your Pet

Richard Webster

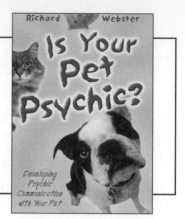

What is your pet thinking?

Cats who predict earthquakes, dogs who improve marriages, and horses who can add and subtract—animals have long been known to possess amazing talents. Now you can experience for yourself the innate psychic abilities of your pet with *Is Your Pet Psychic*.

Learn to exchange ideas with your pet that will enhance your relationship in many ways. Transmit and receive thoughts when you're at a distance, help lost pets find their way home, even communicate with pets who are deceased.

Whether your animal walks, flies, or swims, it is possible to establish a psychic bond and a more meaningful relationship. This book is full of instructions, as well as true case studies from past and present.

0-7387-0193-9
5³⁄₁₆ x 8, 288 pp., bibliog., index $12.95

To order, call 1-877-NEW-WRLD

Prices subject to change without notice